THE PLANT-BASED MEDITERRANEAN DIET COOKBOOK

THE PLANT-BASED MEDITERRANEAN DIET COOKBOOK

75 RECIPES FOR LASTING WEIGHT LOSS AND LIFELONG HEALTH

JENN JODOUIN

Photography by Darren Muir

ROCKRIDGE PRESS

Interior and Cover Designer: Lisa Forde
Art Producer: Janice Ackerman
Editor: Justin Hartung
Production Editor: Mia Moran
Production Manager: Michael Kay

Photography ©2021 Darren Muir. Food styling by Yolanda Muir

Author photo courtesy of Maxine Paquette Photography

ISBN: Print 978-1-64876-453-0
eBook 978-1-64876-454-7

R0

I DEDICATE THIS BOOK
to the changemakers around the
world who are inspiring healthy
living—that includes you!

CONTENTS

INTRODUCTION

My name is Jenn J. I'm an advanced holistic nutritionist and specialize in helping women find relief from the symptoms of underlying hormone imbalances. I'm also a mom, and my journey through motherhood has helped me recognize that for most of my clients, it's impossible to focus on their own health when they're taking care of their family. So I help my clients, and their entire families, push the easy button on their nutrition through simple tools, education, resources, and coaching programs.

I have a very strong belief in the healing power of plant-based foods, as I have personally gained many benefits and watched my clients do the same. But it wasn't always this way, as I, too, used to eat the typical American diet.

My struggles with autoimmune and hormone issues brought me to my knees in my late twenties. At a crossroads in my treatment options, the choices appeared to be medication and menopause, or to seek out the holistic care and support that my body required to feel better.

I opted for the holistic route and have never looked back. Diving into the world of plant-based cooking, I made all of the mistakes that are common in learning a new way of eating, and came out the other side a stronger and healthier version of myself.

A Mediterranean plant-based diet has helped both me and my clients lower the systemic inflammation that causes a lot of body and joint pain and lose excess fat stores and keep them off with ease.

The Mediterranean plant-based diet offers a sustainable, filling, and delicious way to enjoy food every single day without having to weigh portions, restrict calories, or count nutrients. I've seen many of my clients even gain a healthier relationship with their food because of the simple, flexible structure of this diet.

Making changes to your eating habits and lifestyle can be difficult—oftentimes we struggle with knowing what to eat, how to prepare it, and how to manage social functions. In this recipe book, not only will I walk you through the basics of the Mediterranean plant-based diet, but will help make the transition smoother and easier than you might have expected by rounding out the instructions with lots of handy tips, suggestions, and alternatives.

Because I want you to love what you eat and feel amazing, I've included a 14-day meal plan to get you started, along with a guide to stocking and supplying your kitchen. From there, I've provided 75 delicious plant-based Mediterranean recipes to help you sustain your new lifestyle. Good luck!

CHAPTER 1

THE PLANT-BASED MEDITERRANEAN DIET PRIMER

Welcome to your new, healthier life. Here I'll be going over some of the basics of the blended plant-based Mediterranean diet, including definitions, guidelines, health benefits, and tips for success. Changing our diets can be tough, but I'm here to empower you on this journey and encourage your success.

What Is the Mediterranean Diet?

The Mediterranean diet refers to traditions of living and eating in countries around the Mediterranean Sea, drawing from the cooking of Greece, Italy, and Turkey among many others, born from ancient civilizations.

The dietary habits of the people living around the Mediterranean developed from the coastal lands' geography, climate, sands and soils, and length of the growing season, as well as religious beliefs and trade with neighboring countries. Along with seafood, some of the most common foods around the Mediterranean have included dates, figs, almonds, olives, hazelnuts, artichokes, eggplant, potatoes, pomegranates, aromatic herbs, and citrus fruit, plus whole grains found growing in inland regions.

More recently, people around the globe have taken note of the longevity of those living in Mediterranean countries. In 2020, *U.S. News & World Report* published rankings by a panel of nationally recognized health experts, who rated the Mediterranean diet the number one best overall diet.

The Mediterranean diet is now considered one of the most sustainable ways to improve health and lose weight, mainly because:

» It's an easy and flexible diet to follow.
» It offers generous portions and variety.
» It supports a long-term healthy eating pattern.
» It offers documented health benefits when it comes to weight loss, preventing or controlling diabetes, reducing risks of cardiovascular disease, and even promoting good brain health.

Visualizing the Mediterranean diet as a triangle, the large base comprises vegetables, fruits, legumes, whole grains, nuts, seeds, herbs, spices, and extra-virgin olive oil. The upper, smaller part of the triangle includes fish, seafood, dairy, eggs, and poultry, indicating a moderate consumption of these foods. The very tip contains red meat and sweets, which should only be consumed on rare occasions.

While there is no "wrong way" to incorporate it, this diet discourages eating added sugars, processed meats, refined grains, and other highly processed foods.

For a fuller experience that goes beyond food, consider integrating a few more habits that promote good health. Mediterranean-inspired cooking is part of a lifestyle that encourages regular physical activity, sharing meals with others, often enjoying one glass of red wine with dinner, and making water your main drink of choice.

The Plant-Based Connection to the Mediterranean Diet

The Mediterranean diet has often been referred to as a "plant-based way of eating" due to its strong emphasis on eating a wide variety of harvested and foraged foods. In that way, it overlaps with an umbrella of plant-based diets encompassing three main categories: vegetarian, vegan, and whole-food plant-based (WFPB).

While these three diets all have similarities and a strong focus on eating more fruits and vegetables, there are some distinct differences. A vegetarian diet does not include any meat (or fish, when fully adhered to), but could still include dairy and eggs. A vegan diet does not include any animal-based food, ruling out all meat, fish, dairy, eggs, and honey. Still, many versions of these diets allow for processed alternative versions of animal-based foods, such as vegan cheese and lunch meats.

The whole-food plant-based diet focuses on two principles: (1) obtaining nutrition from foods that have not been heavily processed; and (2) obtaining nutrients from foods that are plant-based, while avoiding foods that contain meat, fish, dairy, eggs, or honey.

For some, eating only a vegan or plant-based diet can feel restricting and could lead to nutritional deficiencies in common micronutrients such as iron and vitamins B_{12} and D. Combining the principles from the plant-based and Mediterranean diets can help reduce the risks of nutritional deficiencies, increase the variety of foods enjoyed, and feel less restrictive.

A plant-based diet is considered to be a more environmentally friendly and ethical way of eating, largely because it reduces greenhouse gases and uses less land and water in the growing process.

It's also one of the most sustainable ways to improve your health and lose weight. Devoting more of one's food intake to fruits and vegetables has been shown to prevent, halt, or even reverse chronic disease such as heart disease and type 2 diabetes, and is a logical choice for people looking to correct their health.

In fact, one study conducted on the effects of the combined plant-based Mediterranean diet, published by the National Library of Medicine, showed improved weight loss, a significant decrease in waist circumference, and lower levels of potentially harmful cholesterol compared to the Mediterranean diet alone. The results concluded that a plant-based model, high in fruits, vegetables, and grains and low in meat and poultry, may actually amplify the cardiometabolic effects of the Mediterranean diet.

The Plant-Based Mediterranean Diet, Explained

While a plant-based diet is sometimes viewed as restrictive, the plant-based Mediterranean diet can be easier to follow, as it embodies the colorful variety of the plant-based diet while blending it with the versatility of the Mediterranean diet.

This blended diet is grounded in eating a variety of produce. Both fresh and frozen vegetables and fruits are your best options for health and budget. These tend to contain the highest level of nutrition and are recognized easily by the body for absorption.

Try to eat real, whole foods that are minimally processed. We want to avoid foods that have been altered from their original state—products that contain preservatives, excess salts and sweeteners, and have reduced nutritional value, such as crackers, ready-to-eat meals, and "plant-based meats."

Although red meat is allowed on a Mediterranean diet, it is avoided in the combined plant-based Mediterranean diet.

Instead, enjoy a mix of plant-based proteins and some animal proteins. I'd recommend eating a dish that includes chicken, fish, or eggs just once or twice a week, while focusing on increasing the variety of plant-based proteins like beans, lentils, pulses, and peas.

Dairy, though consumed in moderation on the traditional Mediterranean diet, is discouraged on the plant-based Mediterranean diet. Alternatives to dairy make the transition to plant-based Mediterranean smooth and enjoyable. In this book, in which all the recipes are dairy-free, you'll learn some quick, creative ways to use plant-based alternatives to dairy.

The key to being successful with a plant-based Mediterranean diet is to focus on variety. Aim to have a variety of colors at every meal and throughout the day. This will help with two things: (1) decreasing the likelihood of any nutritional deficiencies; and (2) keeping your meals interesting and fun.

WHOLE-FOOD PLANT-BASED DIET	MEDITERRANEAN DIET	PLANT-BASED MEDITERRANEAN DIET
Enjoy healthy fats	Enjoy eggs, poultry, and dairy in moderation	Enjoy eggs, poultry, and seafood in moderation
Avoid oils	Have red meat on occasion	Avoid red meat
Avoid eggs and dairy	Avoid processed oils	
Avoid seafood		
Avoid meat and poultry		

The Benefits of Going Plant-Based Mediterranean

I've touched lightly on some of the advantages of the plant-based Mediterranean diet when it comes to good health, but let's dive a little deeper into those benefits.

The plant-based Mediterranean diet has been shown to improve cardiovascular health. Your cardiovascular system is responsible for pumping and transporting oxygen-rich blood throughout your body. These two processes work independently but simultaneously to ensure that your body regulates temperature, receives nutrients and hormones, and removes waste products. A healthy cardiovascular system is important in reducing risks of heart disease, high blood pressure, and stroke, which are some of the leading causes of death in the world.

An increased plant intake has been shown to provide significant improvements in gut health. Plant-based foods, including fruits, vegetables, beans, and whole grains, are responsible for providing gut-healing fiber that can improve the quality of our digestive system.

Fiber is a type of carbohydrate that can't be digested by the body, and it has been shown to benefit multiple areas of our health. But many American diets rely heavily on meat, dairy, and highly processed foods, which contain very little fiber. In fact, the average American consumes only 50 percent of the recommended daily amount.

Acting as the body's chimney sweep, fiber can help loosen toxins, excess hormones, waste products, and harmful bacteria from the digestive system and prepare it for elimination. Doing this allows your gastrointestinal (GI) tract to work more efficiently in absorbing nutrients, regulating digestion, and building your immune system. Likewise, with a clean digestive system, the beneficial bacteria that live in your GI tract can grow and flourish. This bacteria thrives only under the right pH conditions, which are created by the enzymatic reactions that take place in your stomach between your digestive juices and the plant-based enzymes known as prebiotics. Prebiotics are generated by plant-based foods.

Both the plant-based and Mediterranean diets are doctor-recommended for diabetes prevention and management. When we have rapid spikes and drops in our blood sugar levels, we feel hungry soon after eating, leading to a habit of overeating and choosing more unhealthy options. The strong focus from both diets on minimally processed foods, reduced refined sugars, and increased fiber intake are particularly helpful in both reducing the risk of developing diabetes and managing type 2 diabetes, as fiber helps regulate your body's use of sugars while also regulating blood glucose (sugar) levels.

Losing weight can actually be a natural by-product on the plant-based Mediterranean diet, without even trying. This is due to the increased fiber intake from plant-based sources of protein that increase feelings of satiety (fullness), and reduce hunger and calorie intake. Animal sources of protein contain little fiber, if any, while a serving of beans can contain as much as 22 grams of fiber. So without having to count calories or feel restricted in your food choices, you could lose excess weight while actually feeling full and not overeating.

You can expect to experience better energy levels on the plant-based Mediterranean diet. Improving your digestion, losing excess weight, and having better-regulated blood sugar levels all improve your chances of having better energy levels and not feeling "bogged down" and heavy.

Some studies show that this blended diet is ideal for optimal health. With an emphasis on the healing powers of plant-based foods, the freedom from restrictions in calories and the reduction of highly processed foods, the plant-based Mediterranean diet is one of the best for achieving and sustaining long-term health.

EAT QUALITY WHOLE-FOOD INGREDIENTS

When food shopping, seek out whole-food and quality ingredients. This means that the food was grown, harvested, and produced to contain the highest levels of nutrition and has passed quality standards. This is often indicated on packaging with labels such as "organic," "free-range," "wild-caught," and "vine-ripened."

Avoid items that contain a long list of ingredients, modified foods, or refined versions of the real thing. Instead, look for a few simple and clean ingredients, low on processing, preservatives, and alterations. For example, choose pasta made from whole-grain flour rather than a type made from refined white flour.

Eating a more plant-based diet is cheaper, given that quality plant proteins like beans and legumes are cheaper than, say, wild-caught salmon. But to keep your produce costs reasonable, buy organic only for the produce that you eat often and that appears on the Environmental Working Group's Dirty Dozen™ list, which is updated annually on the EWG's website.

The Nuts and Olives of the Plant-Based Mediterranean Diet

Let's get down to the nuts and bolts of the plant-based Mediterranean diet—essentially what to eat and what not to eat.

FOODS TO LOVE

Vegetables and dark leafy greens: Vegetables such as cucumbers, peppers, tomatoes, beets, carrots, onions, garlic, spinach, salad greens, cabbage, potatoes, eggplants, artichokes, and asparagus should comprise the bulk of your plate, always. Fresh produce is loaded with antioxidants, vitamins, minerals, and even phytonutrients, and these micronutrients are crucial for healing and protecting your body at a cellular level; they've even been shown to switch your genes/DNA on and off, like light switches, to activate health within the body. Every day, include a variety of dark leafy greens and cruciferous vegetables, such as broccoli, kale, Swiss chard, and Brussels sprouts to increase your dietary calcium sources.

Fruits and berries: Fruits are high in vitamin C, which helps boost the immune system and improve the absorption of plant-based iron. This is important because plant-based iron is not absorbed as efficiently as animal-based sources. So enjoy plenty of apples, bananas, melons, dried fruits, dates, figs, apricots, cherries, peaches, oranges, plums, kiwis, lemons, limes, mangos, papayas, pineapples, olives, and all berries.

Whole grains: Refined grains that have been heavily processed (such as white flour, which has been stripped of the husk and bran) don't have as many nutrients as whole grains, such as wild rice, whole wheat bread and pasta, quinoa, couscous, bulgur, oats, buckwheat, millet, barley, spelt, farro, and even corn. Whole grains should be a staple in your house, as they're typically high in protein, iron, zinc, B vitamins, magnesium, selenium, and phosphorus. These micronutrients are crucial for energy levels, healthy hair and skin, immune system support, and muscle function.

Beans and legumes: A great source of plant-based protein, iron, potassium, and folate, beans and legumes help keep you full and satiated, so you don't feel the need to overeat. Studies have also shown that eating more legumes, such as black beans, chickpeas, and lentils, can lower blood pressure and blood sugar and reduce the risk of heart disease.

Nuts and seeds: While nuts and seeds are higher in calories and lower in fiber than some other foods, they are an important part of this blended way of eating. A source of healthy fats, they help stabilize blood sugar without increasing the risk of cardiovascular disease. Walnuts, hemp hearts, chia seeds, and flaxseed are excellent sources of omega-3 fatty acids, which have been shown to reduce inflammation, support brain function, and promote a healthy mood. Your body cannot create these types of fats, and so you must rely on your diet to obtain them. On a regular Mediterranean diet, omega-3s are primarily covered by seafood. In this blended diet, however, with its focus on plant-based nutrition, nuts and seeds fit the bill. Keep a variety on hand, like almonds, cashews, pumpkin seeds, macadamia nuts, sunflower seeds, and Brazil nuts for different flavors and textures.

Oils and spices: This category helps you to add life and zest to your food. Extra-virgin olive oil, which enriches cooked dishes and salads, can be enjoyed in small amounts (around 2 tablespoons per day); this minimally processed oil contains heart-healthy vitamin E, proven to reduce the risk of cardiovascular disease and inflammation. And spices from around the world not only enhance your cooking, many of them (such as turmeric, ginger, and garlic) contain anti-inflammatory properties that can improve your overall health and well-being.

FOODS TO LIMIT AND LET GO

Fish, poultry, and eggs: Stick to only one or two servings a week containing an ingredient from this whole group of foods. To get the full benefits of this blended diet, you really want to focus on increasing your consumption of plant-based protein sources.

Dairy and cheese: A gray area of the combined diet, dairy and cheese have been shown to increase inflammation within the body, interfere with natural hormone production and regulation, and may contain processed ingredients. This book will help you get comfortable with—and even savor—the plant-based alternatives to dairy.

Red meats: Avoid red meat, like beef. Consumption of red meat has been linked to increased risks of cardiovascular diseases and is unnecessary when eating a varied plant-based diet.

Processed foods: Avoid these, many of which come in the form of heat-up meals, canned soups, jarred sauces, and packaged snacks. They contain little nutritional value and instead are full of harmful additives that contribute to poor health.

Refined sugars: Avoid white sugar, brown sugar, sugary syrups, and high-fructose corn syrup. These refined sugars contribute to increased inflammation within the body, risks of type 2 diabetes, and insulin resistance. Honey is not technically plant-based, but is also not refined. In moderation, honey is acceptable as long as you're not following a vegan diet.

YOUR PLANT-BASED MEDITERRANEAN CHEAT SHEET

Fruits and Vegetables
All fresh and frozen, as well as fermented

Grains, Flours, and Legumes
Whole wheat flour, whole-grain flour, whole-grain bread and pasta, brown rice, couscous, quinoa, wild rice, farro, whole oats, steel-cut oats, oat flour, spelt, black beans, chickpeas, kidney beans, cannellini beans, lentils, black-eyed peas

Dairy
Plant-based yogurt and milks

Nuts and Seeds
Hemp hearts, chia seeds, flaxseed, walnuts, almonds, macadamia nuts, Brazil nuts, pecans, cashews, pumpkin seeds, sunflower seeds, sesame seeds, tahini and other nut/seed butters, almond flour

Fats and Oils
Extra-virgin olive oil, avocado, coconut

Sweeteners, Spices, and Seasonings
Fresh and dried herbs and spices (e.g., basil, parsley, oregano, garlic, onion, cardamom, turmeric, cumin, saffron, cilantro, dill, fennel, nutmeg, cinnamon, paprika, tarragon, thyme, curry powder, vanilla, sea salt, black pepper), balsamic vinegar, apple cider vinegar, rice wine vinegar, red wine vinegar, white vinegar

Beverages
Water, herbal tea

EAT IN MODERATION

Fruits and Vegetables
Unsweetened, dried fruits (e.g., raisins, dried cranberries, dried cherries)

Grains, Flours, and Legumes
Quick-cooking oats, 50/50 baking flours

Animal Protein
Fish, seafood, poultry, eggs

Dairy
Animals' milk/yogurt; cheese common in Mediterranean countries, such as feta, ricotta, and Parmesan

Nuts and Seeds
Peanuts, peanut butter

Fats and Oils
Ghee, butter

Sweeteners, Spices, and Seasonings
Honey, date syrup, molasses, pure maple syrup, stevia leaf extract

Beverages
Red wine, 100% real fruit and veggie juices, tea, black coffee, plain seltzer water

AVOID

Grains, Flours, and Legumes
Refined white flour, white bread, pasta (unless whole-grain), white rice, vegan meat-alternatives

Animal Protein
Red meat (beef, pork, lamb)

Dairy
Sweetened dairy products (e.g., commercial fruit yogurt); processed cheese (e.g., Velveeta, vegan cheese-alternatives)

Fats and Oils
Processed/refined vegetable oils (e.g., corn oil, canola oil, margarine)

Sweeteners, Spices, and Seasonings
Processed sauces (e.g., Cheez Whiz) and dressing/seasoning mix packets (e.g., ranch dressing mix), refined sugar (e.g., white/brown sugar, corn syrup, table syrup)

Beverages
Fruit juice blends, alcoholic drinks, carbonated/caffeinated/sweetened drinks, energy drinks, meal replacement drinks

Stocking Your Plant-Based Mediterranean Kitchen

While you won't need anything too unusual to succeed with the diet, there are a few essential food items and kitchen tools you should have on hand to make the recipes in this book.

PANTRY AND COUNTER

Oats: You can use rolled, quick, or minute oats in breakfast, lunch, dinner, and baking recipes.

Nutritional yeast: Different from baker's yeast, nutritional yeast provides a dairy-free, cheesy flavor, and will become your best friend to replace dairy-based cheese.

Whole grains: Stock up on quinoa, couscous, bulgur, farro, spelt, buckwheat, and wild rice.

Legumes: Opt for chickpeas, black turtle beans, red kidney beans, Romano beans (Italian flat beans), white cannellini beans, brown lentils, and red lentils.

Dried herbs and spices: You can easily change a recipe from Italian to Moroccan with spices alone. Stock up on basil, parsley, oregano, thyme, tarragon, garlic, onion, cumin, curry, turmeric, nutmeg, dill, and cinnamon. Whenever possible, make your own spice blends in bulk to avoid using store-bought options that may contain additives, preservatives, and unnecessary sodium.

Vinegars: The ones you'll use the most are balsamic and apple cider vinegar. Most of them can be used interchangeably, so don't worry if you only have one on hand.

Extra-virgin olive oil: Use it to make dressings, to sauté and roast vegetables, and to thin out your dips.

Seeds: Both flaxseed and chia seeds can be used in baking to replace eggs, while hemp hearts and sesame seeds, pumpkin seeds, and sunflower seeds pack a nutritional punch.

Nuts: Walnuts, almonds, and cashews always make a quick snack, and can be excellent toppings for salads and soups.

Flours: Whole-grain, oat flour, coconut flour, almond flour, and multigrain (whole) flours are some of the varieties I use most, but you can usually get away with just a good-quality whole wheat or oat flour.

Sweeteners: Keep just a few available and use them sparingly. Pure maple syrup will be the predominant sweetener in this book, though you can exchange it for some of the sweeteners listed in the cheat sheet.

Nut and seed butters: Tahini, a spread made of only blended sesame seeds, is a common ingredient in Mediterranean dishes, and is used often in this book's recipes.

REFRIGERATOR AND FREEZER

Frozen vegetables: These can help you eat a larger variety of vegetables as the seasons change. Try keeping broccoli, cauliflower, carrots, peas, Brussels sprouts, beets, and squash in your freezer to add a colorful touch to every meal.

Frozen fruits: These are a great way to make desserts, snacks, and breakfasts easier, more nutritious, and less expensive. Frozen berries, peaches, pineapples, cherries, and bananas are some of my favorites.

Leafy greens: Try two to three varieties each week for a well-rounded source of nutrition. Some top picks are spinach, kale, Swiss chard, collards, romaine lettuce, and bok choy.

Onions: I like both red and white onions. White onions are a go-to for cooked meals, while red onions can be enjoyed raw in many Mediterranean dishes.

Garlic: Closely related to the onion, garlic has flavor compounds that help bring out and enhance the flavors of other foods.

Plant-based milk: Dairy-free milk alternatives are made by soaking a nut seed, or grain in water, blending it together, and straining out the pulp; given the time-consuming process, store-bought is a great way to go. Almond, cashew, and soy milks are similar to 2% cow's milk; while rice, oat, and coconut milk (from a carton) are similar to 1% cow's milk. Choose unsweetened milks that are fortified with nutrition important for plant-based diets, such as calcium, folate, vitamin D, and magnesium. I prefer to use almond milk, but feel free to use your favorite.

Fresh fruit: Keep a rainbow selection of fruit on hand for snacking and desserts, such as bananas, apples, grapes, peaches, and oranges.

Fresh vegetables: Since vegetables are the star of plant-based Mediterranean cuisine, be sure to keep a colorful selection of your favorites, and aim to try one new variety, color, or flavor on a regular basis. My refrigerator is often stocked with cucumbers, peppers, tomatoes, broccoli, zucchini, and root vegetables, like sweet potato, beets, and carrots.

Culture-rich foods: Feeding your gut healthy bacteria is easier with foods rich in probiotics. Choose plant-based cultured yogurts, water kefir, and kombucha, as well as fermented foods like sauerkraut, from the refrigerated section of your grocery store.

Plant-based yogurt: Plant-based yogurts are dairy-free, usually vegan, and made from coconut, almond, or cashew bases. Choose unsweetened options.

Fresh herbs: Bring a little sparkle to Mediterranean dips, sauces, and dishes with fresh herbs like parsley, cilantro, basil, and dill.

ESSENTIAL EQUIPMENT

Cutting board: I'd recommend having two distinct cutting boards—one specifically for animal proteins, and one for everything else. Plastic boards wash nicely and don't harbor bacteria in the same way wooden boards do.

Set of knives: This is a must in plant-based eating to cut down on prep time. You will be chopping, dicing, mincing, and slicing plenty of vegetables for your meals, so invest in a set of sharp knives, or three basic knives: a good chef's knife, a paring knife, and a Santoku knife. Also use a blade sharpener.

Veggie peeler: Find one that's sharp, comfortable to hold, and easy to use.

Powerful blender: Smoothies, sauces, dips, and other fun recipes come together quickly and mess-free in a blender.

Steamer basket: Steaming your vegetables, rather than boiling, can help to retain sensitive water-soluble vitamins (such as vitamins B and C).

Skillet: Choose a medium pan, such as a stainless-steel or a nonstick pan, that heats up well and distributes heat evenly.

Roasting tray: Choose a tray with a lip that is a ½ inch to 1 inch in height, to be sure that it will hold in any sauces or drippings.

Can opener: Electric or manual, a can opener will be a lifesaver for you throughout this book, as we will be using precooked, canned beans to reduce time in the kitchen.

Spiralizer: Adding more vegetables to our plate sometimes requires a little bit of creativity, so a spiralizer can come in handy. This tool will help us make some veggie-based alternatives to traditional favorites, like pastas.

Whisk: This tool is great for blending dressings, sauces, and dips and preparing the occasional egg dish.

PUTTING THE LIFE IN HEALTHY LIFESTYLE

Leading a healthy lifestyle—not just eating nutritiously—is a big part of the Mediterranean diet. So when making a shift in diet, other lifestyle changes shouldn't be an afterthought—they can be planned with, and around, your food. Try adding some of these healthy habits to your routine, and enjoy the holistic benefits they bring you:

» Eating with other people has been shown to promote more sensible eating habits, which can help support both you and your loved ones.

» Reduce distractions (like TV or phones) while eating. Doing so can improve your chances of being more in tune with your body, and understanding the satiety cues to stop eating when you're full.

» Chew your food longer and savor the flavors and textures while you eat—this can improve your digestion, as digestion actually begins in the mouth, and can keep you from overeating.

» Take a walk to get some exercise and fresh air. Regular exercise and movement can lower risks of cardiovascular disease and obesity, and even improve your sleep. Fresh air (and sun exposure) can help with mood regulation while improving energy levels and mental focus, as well as digestion. Consider taking a brisk walk after eating a meal.

» Turn off your screens 30 to 60 minutes before bed to improve the quality of your sleep. The white-blue lights from our devices have been shown to interfere with our body's ability to release and regulate melatonin, our sleep hormone, which results in decreased sleep quality and indirectly heightens our cortisol (stress) levels and fat production/retention.

» Make time for your hobbies. Along with being gratifying, they're important for restoring energy, reducing stress, elevating endorphins (your feel-good hormones) and improving your mental health.

What to Expect on the Plant-Based Mediterranean Diet

A "clean" diet is one that's low in refined sugars and processed foods. Depending on how "clean" your diet currently is, you may experience some rapid changes or some more long-term sustained results in your weight and health as you begin this new way of eating.

If you're not currently eating a clean diet, you can likely expect to see some weight loss and increased energy levels within just a few weeks of starting. If your diet is pretty clean right now, and you're enhancing it through this transition, then you can expect to experience incremental changes in your weight and health over time.

Either way, this book will provide you with a plan for long-term sustained health and weight maintenance. Every day that you eat the plant-based Mediterranean diet gets you closer to your ideal weight and optimal health.

In this journey, I speak from experience when I say that you will come to moments that are tough, confusing, or overwhelming. Some of the toughest moments in transitioning to a new way of eating present themselves in the very beginning. One of the biggest struggles my clients face at this stage is not knowing what to make for a meal, or how to include plant-based proteins in a meal they're comfortable and familiar with.

Don't despair. In the next chapter, not only will you have a 14-day menu to jump-start your success, but I'm going to help you stay successful beyond the first 14 days by walking you through some simple, yet effective ways to overcome those challenging moments.

About the Recipes

The recipes and their flavor profiles take inspiration from countries all over the Mediterranean, from western Italy to eastern Israel to southern Morocco and northern Greece, and all the countries in between that share a coast along the Mediterranean Sea. I've tried to include a variety of flavors to show you how versatile and fun plant-based eating can be.

You can also expect to cook some plant-based alternatives to American favorites, while keeping in line with the Mediterranean-style guidelines. Having some comforting recipes and meals with a healthier plant-based Mediterranean spin can really help you enjoy the transition.

Making the change to a new way of eating can be challenging. So to keep it easy and achievable, I've included recipes that contain fewer than 10 ingredients whenever possible, that require a limited amount of preparation and cooking time, and that contain accessible ingredients found in most grocery stores.

Note that while all of the ingredients I've included work for the Mediterranean plant-based diet, they may not all agree with each individual. To modify the recipes, I've tried to provide a few alternatives to the more common allergen ingredients, but if you find that a certain food doesn't sit well with you, try avoiding it for a few weeks and subbing in something else. It can be helpful to keep a food journal when trying new recipes in order to track any patterns that may emerge in how you feel.

You'll find some additional guidance in the labels and tips included with the recipes. For example, recipes may be labeled "Gluten-Free" or "Quick" at the top, allowing you to identify important information about the meal without reading the whole page. Tips at the bottom, on topics such as preparation, variations, and leftovers, will help you adjust or modify the recipe to suit your preferences, and save money and time.

CHAPTER 2

14-DAY JUMP-START PLAN AND BEYOND

Welcome to the first 14 days of your new adventure! In this chapter you're going to find two meal plans, each spanning one week. The purpose of this jump-start plan is to give you the best chance of success and show you how to assemble a simple day's worth of meals to maximize your nutrition intake, weight loss, and health goals.

Following the two-week plan, we'll dive into some tips for ongoing success, starting with goal setting, meal planning, eating out, and managing cravings. We're going to be wrapping up this chapter with a warm hug as we discuss the importance of self-compassion on your journey.

About the Plan

On the following pages are meal plans laid out in a simple table that, when read from left to right, will show you the meals for the entire day.

The meal plans, which are designed for two people, include breakfast, lunch, and dinner for each day of the week. Recipe titles that are printed in *italics* indicate that they are leftovers from earlier meals and do not need to be made a second time.

Each day is designed to meet your nutritional requirements and is around 1,700 calories, which helps reinforce your weight-loss goals when combined with a light-to-moderate fitness routine, and yet leave you full and satisfied.

I have included a variety of hot and cold dishes, as well as meals that take very little time to prepare. Some meals have leftovers for another day's meal. This is to reduce time in the kitchen and avoid needing to restock your supplies after one week.

These dishes can be scaled with ease. For example, if you're feeding a family of four you can double each recipe. If you're dining solo, you can halve the recipe or save the leftovers; most leftovers can be stored in an airtight container in the refrigerator for three to five days, and some can even be stored in the freezer for two to three months.

In some recipes, substitutions can be made based on what you have on hand. Some of the simplest substitutions are any dark leafy green in place of another, whole grains in place of other whole grains, and using dried and fresh herbs interchangeably.

INCORPORATING SNACKS AND SWEETS

You'll notice that the meal plans do not contain snacks or desserts. That's because I want you to focus on the core meals to get you off to a strong start in your new, healthy diet.

Between meals, snacks and desserts serve the role of filling in some nutritional gaps and acting as energy boosters and craving crushers. A healthy snack can be an excellent way to sustain energy levels and curb hunger pangs during the day. Desserts are encouraged in moderation as part of a healthy, balanced lifestyle. Check out the recipes in chapter 8 for some great snack and dessert options.

In the meantime, if you're hungry between meals, try some celery sticks with 1 tablespoon of nut butter, ½ cup of unsweetened plant-based yogurt and berries, or 2 tablespoons of hummus with carrot sticks.

Week I

Are you ready to get started? During this week, you can expect to have dinner leftovers for the majority of your lunches and new meals every night of the week. This allows you to reuse many of your ingredients without stressing about making three different meals every day. The weekday breakfasts come together in just a few minutes, while you can expect breakfasts on the weekend to take a little longer.

Week 1

	BREAKFAST	LUNCH	DINNER
MONDAY	Toast with ½ mashed avocado	Tomato Bisque (page 56)	Broccoli and Chickpea Couscous (page 90)
TUESDAY	Berry and Nut No-Cereal Bowl (page 38)	*Leftover Broccoli and Chickpea Couscous*	*Leftover Tomato Bisque*
WEDNESDAY	Raspberry Zesty Smoothie (page 35)	Veggie Pita Pizza with Hummus (page 69)	Mediterranean Buddha Bowl (page 76) with Tzatziki (page 130)
THURSDAY	Toast with ½ mashed avocado	*Leftover Buddha Bowl with leftover Tzatziki*	One-Pan Chicken, Broccoli, and Peppers (page 101)
FRIDAY	Berry and Nut No-Cereal Bowl (page 38)	*Leftover One-Pan Chicken, Broccoli, and Peppers*	Three-Bean Chili (page 91)
SATURDAY	Banana-Nut Overnight Oats (page 37)	*Leftover Three-Bean Chili*	One-Pan Rosemary-Roasted Tofu (page 84) and Roasted Garlic and Cauliflower Mash (page 85)
SUNDAY	Tofu Scramble (page 45)	*Leftover One-Pan Rosemary Roasted Tofu and Roasted Garlic-Cauliflower Mash*	Clear out the refrigerator

WEEK 1 SHOPPING LIST

PRODUCE

- [ ] Avocado
- [ ] Baby spinach
- [ ] Basil, fresh
- [ ] Bananas
- [ ] Bell peppers (green and orange)
- [ ] Blackberries (fresh or frozen)
- [ ] Celery
- [ ] Cherry tomatoes
- [ ] Cucumbers
- [ ] Garlic
- [ ] Lemons
- [ ] Mixed greens
- [ ] Mushrooms
- [ ] Parsley, fresh
- [ ] Raspberries, fresh or frozen
- [ ] Red onions
- [ ] Strawberries, fresh or frozen
- [ ] White onions
- [ ] Yellow onions
- [ ] Zucchini

BREADS/GRAINS

- [ ] Couscous
- [ ] Quinoa
- [ ] Whole-grain bread
- [ ] Whole wheat pita

PANTRY

- [ ] 3-Bean Medley (16-ounce can)
- [ ] Almonds, raw
- [ ] Apple cider vinegar
- [ ] Black salt (optional)
- [ ] Canned diced tomatoes
- [ ] Cannellini beans
- [ ] Chia seeds
- [ ] Chickpeas
- [ ] Chili powder
- [ ] Cinnamon, ground
- [ ] Cornstarch
- [ ] Cumin
- [ ] Dijon mustard (whole-grain)
- [ ] Dill, dried
- [ ] Extra-virgin olive oil
- [ ] Garlic powder
- [ ] Hemp hearts
- [ ] Maple syrup
- [ ] Nutmeg, ground
- [ ] Nutritional yeast
- [ ] Olives (kalamata, black, green, pitted)
- [ ] Paprika
- [ ] Pumpkin seeds
- [ ] Rosemary, dried
- [ ] Sea salt
- [ ] Soy sauce (reduced-sodium)
- [ ] Thyme, dried
- [ ] Tomato paste (4-ounce can)
- [ ] Turmeric
- [ ] Vanilla extract

Continued >

- ☐ Vegetable broth (or make your own, page 123)
- ☐ Walnuts, unsalted
- ☐ White wine vinegar
- ☐ Whole oats

REFRIGERATED/ FROZEN

- ☐ Broccoli
- ☐ Cauliflower
- ☐ Chicken breasts

- ☐ Tofu, extra-firm, (14-ounce package)
- ☐ Unsweetened non-dairy milk

PREP AHEAD

Get ready for your week by prepping a few items ahead of time.

1. Prep a batch of Tzatziki (page 130) for your Buddha Bowls and store in an airtight container in the refrigerator.

2. Prep your Raspberry Zesty Smoothies (page 35) ahead of time by portioning out the ingredients into individual-serving smoothie bags. Freeze the bags until ready to use. Do not add the liquid yet, you'll do this the day you're making the smoothie.

3. Cook the quinoa (and brown rice, if using). Allow the grains to cool before putting them into airtight containers in the refrigerator.

4. If you have a little bit of extra time, cut your peppers into strips, peel and shred your carrots, and seed and dice the cucumber. (Purchase English cucumber to skip the seeding step.) Store each prepared vegetable in separate airtight containers in the refrigerator.

Week 2

	BREAKFAST	LUNCH	DINNER
MONDAY	Green Smoothie (page 34)	*Leftover Tofu Scramble Wrap from Week 1*	One-Pot Whitefish and Rice (page 95)
TUESDAY	Toast with Strawberry-Chia Jam (page 129)	*Leftover One-Pot Whitefish and Rice*	Pasta with Lentil-Beet Balls (page 78)
WEDNESDAY	Green Smoothie (page 34)	Veggie Pita Pizza with Hummus	Minestrone (page 59)
THURSDAY	Toast with Strawberry-Chia Jam (page 129)	*Leftover Minestrone*	Cranberry, Broccoli, and Quinoa Salad (page 52)
FRIDAY	Figs and Tofu Yogurt with Flaxseed (page 39)	*Leftover Cranberry, Broccoli, and Quinoa Salad*	Pesto Shrimp Pasta (page 98)
SATURDAY	Kale and Red Pepper Frittata (page 41)	*Leftover Pesto Shrimp Pasta*	White Bean Zucchini Alfredo (page 77)
SUNDAY	Tofu Shakshuka (page 42)	*Leftover Kale and Red Pepper Frittata in a Wrap*	Clear out the refrigerator

WEEK 2 SHOPPING LIST

PRODUCE

- Avocado
- Baby spinach, fresh
- Banana
- Basil, fresh
- Beet, large
- Bell peppers (red, yellow, green)
- Broccoli, fresh
- Carrots
- Cherry tomatoes
- Cucumber
- Figs
- Garlic
- Green zucchini
- Kale leaves, fresh
- Lemons
- Orange
- Parsley, fresh
- Scallions
- Strawberries
- Yellow onion

BREADS/GRAINS

- Quinoa
- Whole-grain basmati rice
- Whole-grain fettuccine
- Whole-grain pasta
- Whole-grain tortillas
- Whole oats
- Whole wheat/ whole-grain bread

PANTRY

- Apple cider vinegar
- Basil, dried
- Cannellini beans (16-ounce can)
- Cashews, raw
- Chia seeds
- Chili flakes
- Coriander
- Cranberries, dried and unsweetened
- Cumin
- Diced tomatoes, fire-roasted (16-ounce can)
- Dijon mustard (whole-grain)
- Extra-virgin olive oil
- Garlic powder
- Ground flaxseed
- Hemp hearts
- Maple syrup
- Nutritional yeast
- Olives (kalamata, green, pitted)
- Oregano, dried
- Paprika
- Parsley, dried
- Pumpkin seeds, shelled
- Red lentils (16-ounce can)
- Sunflower seeds, shelled
- Tomato paste
- Tomato sauce (12-ounce can)

REFRIGERATOR/ FREEZER

- ☐ Eggs
- ☐ Frozen bananas
- ☐ Frozen green beans
- ☐ Haddock fillets
- ☐ Shrimp
- ☐ Tofu, extra-firm (14-ounce package)
- ☐ Tofu, silken (14-ounce package)
- ☐ Unsweetened non-dairy milk

PREP-AHEAD ADVICE

Let's have you feeling like a pro in the kitchen this week. Start the menu by following these prep tips at the beginning of the week:

1. Prepare and cook the lentil-beet balls (see page 78) to reduce kitchen time later in the week. Cool them and then store in the refrigerator until needed.

2. Make the Strawberry-Chia Jam (page 129) and store in the refrigerator for the week.

3. Package your Green Smoothie (page 34) ingredients (except the liquid) into individual serving-size freezer bags and freeze until you're ready to use them.

4. Chop the peppers, carrots, cucumber, tomatoes, and broccoli, and store in individual containers in the refrigerator.

Beyond the First 14 Days

Congratulations! You've just made it through the first 14 days, the hardest part of your new journey. I strongly urge you to celebrate your victories over the last two weeks—both big and small.

This section is going to give you guidance on how to make this diet work for you in the long term.

SET SMART GOALS

The first part of being successful in anything in life is setting goals. I really love the SMART method for goal-setting and use it with all of my clients in the onboarding and evaluation process. "SMART" is an acronym for a goal that is "Specific, Measurable, Attainable, Realistic, and Time-Based."

Use this acronym to break down the details of your goal and set your expectations, so that you can keep up the good habits you've started for the long haul.

Be very specific. The more specific you are in the details of the what, how, and why of your goals, the easier they will be to track, adjust, and achieve.

Write down your goals. Then put them somewhere so you'll see them all of the time, like your screensaver, your refrigerator door, your bathroom mirror, or even in your car.

Keep a food journal. A food journal is a great way to track your meals, including how they make you feel, and recognize patterns in how or what you're eating that may cause you to fall offtrack. One of my favorite reasons for doing this is that you now have a list of the meals you've eaten and can mark the ones that are favorites, so if you ever hit a slump in knowing what dishes to make, you can refer back to your journal and find the ones you loved.

Be honest with yourself. It's fine to dream big, but don't set yourself up for failure by setting unrealistic expectations of yourself, your time, and your abilities. Be honest about what you can commit to and write your goals around that.

PLAN YOUR MEALS

Planning your meals is the next most important part of success. The work you do ahead of time will help you stick to this diet in an accessible, affordable way.

Make a meal plan based on what you already have in the pantry, refrigerator, and freezer. This type of meal planning will save you time and money and ensure that nothing goes to waste, while encouraging you to be creative with what you have on hand.

Plan to eat leftovers on the days you expect to be the busiest. This allows you to be eating a meal within five minutes of pulling it from the refrigerator.

It's perfectly okay to repeat some meals a few days a week. Don't feel like you need to have a different breakfast, lunch, and dinner every day of the week. Most of us just don't have the kind of time required to eat like this.

Repurpose and reuse some ingredients in different meals. For example, if a recipe calls for pumpkin but you're eating sweet potatoes in another meal that week, just use sweet potatoes for your pumpkin recipe. Other leftovers, like a lentil chili, can be repurposed on a plate of pasta as a sauce.

DINING OUT AND MANAGING CRAVINGS

Dining out, at a restaurant or any social function, can be the most challenging hurdle of all, so prepare for success by remembering a few simple tips.

Look online or call ahead. Most restaurants have their menu posted on their website, so you can choose a healthy meal before your hunger kicks in.

Ask for a modification. Many restaurants are willing to accommodate some simple changes in a dish, such as adding a plant-based burger, instead of chicken strips, on top of a salad.

Bring your own. If you're going to a social function, bring one of your favorite and most satisfying plant-based Mediterranean meals. Who knows? It could be the hit of the party.

Choose international. Cuisines like Italian, Greek, and Mexican are likely to have some healthy plant-based meals (especially when you modify them). So when dining out, choose a cuisine that will naturally have plenty of healthy options.

HAVING SELF-COMPASSION

Switching to a new diet is hard. Have self-compassion on your journey and know that some days are going to be better than others. Understanding ahead of time that you won't always get it perfect can help you keep reasonable expectations of yourself. Remember, you're taking on this new way of eating because it has flexibility, so be forgiving with yourself. If you fall off the wagon, don't beat yourself up; acknowledge how you could have handled the situation differently, and move on to your next meal.

Raspberry Zesty
Smoothie,
page **35**

CHAPTER 3

SMOOTHIES, BREAKFAST, AND BRUNCH

GREEN SMOOTHIE

QUICK

SERVES 1
PREP TIME: 5 minutes

1 banana, frozen
¼ cup rolled or quick oats
2 tablespoons
   hemp hearts
1 cup baby spinach
1 cup unsweetened
   nondairy milk

A healthy, filling breakfast doesn't get easier than a smoothie. Smoothies are one of the quickest options that you can throw together for a meal on the go, and can pack a powerful nutrition punch, all while hiding a few extra servings of vegetables. For these reasons, this simple smoothie recipe is showing up first.

1. Place the banana, oats, hemp hearts, spinach, and milk in a blender.

2. Blend until smooth.

3. Drink and enjoy as soon as possible.

INGREDIENT TIP: While oats are naturally gluten-free, often-times they are processed in the same facilities as wheat, rye, and barley, and cross-contamination can be of concern for people who are sensitive to gluten. Use oats that have a gluten-free label if you're concerned about a sensitivity.

PREP TIP: If you don't have frozen bananas, you can use a ripe banana and add 2 to 4 ice cubes to give your smoothie the same cold, creamy texture.

VARIATION TIP: Round out the nutrition in this basic smoothie by adding half an avocado for balanced blood sugar and energy levels; ½ teaspoon cinnamon to help curb sweet cravings; or even 1 to 2 tablespoons of chia seeds or ground flaxseed for extra fiber.

PER SERVING: Calories: 352; Total fat: 15g; Saturated fat: 1g; Sodium: 199mg; Carbohydrates: 46g; Fiber: 7g; Sugar: 17g; Protein: 13g

RASPBERRY ZESTY SMOOTHIE

GLUTEN-FREE, QUICK

SERVES 1
PREP TIME: 5 minutes

1 cup frozen cauliflower
1 cup frozen raspberries,
Juice of 1 lemon
¼ cup hemp hearts
1 tablespoon chia seeds
1 teaspoon vanilla extract
1½ cups unsweetened
   nondairy milk

Since not everyone is a huge fan of green smoothies, I came up with this recipe for a whole different flavor and color. The chia seeds and hemp hearts add a nice boost of protein to keep you feeling full for several hours. Meanwhile, the raspberries and lemon juice hide the taste of the cauliflower, meaning you won't even notice you're getting an extra serving of vegetables. Smoothies tend to lose their color and texture over time due to the enzymatic reactions of the fruits and vegetables, so aim to drink them within 30 minutes of blending them.

1. In a powerful blender, combine the cauliflower, raspberries, lemon juice, hemp hearts, chia seeds, vanilla, and milk.

2. Blend until smooth.

3. Drink as soon as possible.

VARIATION TIP: Frozen cauliflower is lightly steamed before being frozen, so it has a very mild flavor. If that gives the recipe a little too much "zing" for you, add half a frozen ripe banana to sweeten and soften the taste. If you're using fresh cauliflower, you may want to lightly steam it and let it cool before blending into the smoothie.

PER SERVING: Calories: 525; Total fat: 28g; Saturated fat: 2g; Sodium: 302mg; Carbohydrates: 54g; Fiber: 21g; Sugar: 24g; Protein: 22g

CHIA SEED PUDDING WITH APPLES

GLUTEN-FREE, QUICK

SERVES 1
PREP TIME: 5 minutes,
plus 10 minutes to set

3 tablespoons chia seeds
¾ cup unsweetened
  nondairy milk
¼ teaspoon ground
  cinnamon
1 apple, cored and diced
2 tablespoons pecans

Although you may think of rice pudding as a dessert, it's not uncommon to eat it for breakfast in Italy and other countries. This variation swaps in healthy chia seeds for the rice. Chia seeds are a nutritional power-house that pack a whopping 20 percent of your daily calcium requirements in just 3 tablespoons, and are high in other nutrients, such as protein, potassium, iron, and omega-3 fatty acids.

1. In a cereal bowl, large mug, or canning jar, mix the chia seeds and milk and let set for 10 minutes.

2. Add the cinnamon, apple, and pecans to the chia seed and milk mixture, stir together and enjoy.

PREP TIP: Use small glass canning jars to make enough of these for every day of the week and use some of the options in the Variation Tip to increase variety for the week. These will keep in the refrigerator for 4 to 5 days, and since they'll continue to thicken, be sure to add a splash of milk when you're ready to eat them.

VARIATION TIP: I love the apple and cinnamon in this recipe, but a few other delicious pairings to try are blueberries and vanilla extract; pineapple chunks with shredded coconut; peanut butter and bananas; or cherries with some unsweet-ened dark chocolate.

PER SERVING: Calories: 397; Total fat: 22g; Saturated fat: 1g; Sodium: 132mg; Carbohydrates: 45g; Fiber: 21g; Sugar: 21g; Protein: 9g

BANANA-NUT OVERNIGHT OATS

SERVES 1

PREP TIME: 5 minutes, plus 4 to 8 hours to set

¼ cup rolled or quick oats

⅓ cup unsweetened nondairy milk

½ teaspoon ground cinnamon

⅛ teaspoon ground nutmeg

¼ teaspoon vanilla extract

1 tablespoon maple syrup

¼ cup chopped walnuts

1 banana, sliced

There are a lot of benefits in having a hearty breakfast, but I know how tough that can be on busy days. The oatmeal in this recipe is ready when the milk is absorbed and all of the oats are soft, which usually takes about 4 hours, but as the name says, you can keep it in the refrigerator overnight. In fact, you can even make several servings earlier in the week for a super easy breakfast.

1. In a container with an airtight lid, mix the oats, milk, cinnamon, nutmeg, vanilla, and maple syrup.

2. Add the walnuts and banana to the oatmeal and fold them in.

3. Seal the container and place in the refrigerator and let chill for at least 4 hours or overnight.

PREP TIP: You do not have to precook the oats. As long as you're using rolled or quick oats, they'll absorb the milk and "cook" overnight. So you can have this meal the next day straight out of the refrigerator, or warm it up for some comfort.

LEFTOVERS TIP: If you have some left at the end of the week, add more fruit and milk and blend it into a smoothie.

PER SERVING: Calories: 442; Total fat: 22g; Saturated fat: 2g; Sodium: 63mg; Carbohydrates: 60g; Fiber: 8g; Sugar: 28g; Protein: 9g

BERRY AND NUT NO-CEREAL BOWL

SERVES 1
PREP TIME: 5 minutes

½ cup sliced strawberries
½ cup blackberries
2 tablespoons
  chopped walnuts
2 tablespoons
  chopped almonds
1 tablespoon
  pumpkin seeds
1 tablespoon hemp hearts
¼ to ½ cup unsweetened
  nondairy milk

For an update on the traditional cereal breakfast, try this berry and nut breakfast bowl. The healthy fats from the nuts and seeds help to stabilize blood sugar levels and provide energy. It's the perfect midweek option to get you ready for a busy day and keep you feeling satiated. The fruits in this recipe can be fresh or frozen, slightly or fully thawed. Save money by buying frozen berries in large bulk bags.

1. In a cereal bowl, combine the strawberries, blackberries, walnuts, almonds, pumpkin seeds, and hemp hearts.

2. Pour the milk over the cereal and enjoy.

INGREDIENT TIP: Feel free to use any unsweetened, plant-based milk you prefer, such as cashew, soy, rice, or oat. You can adjust the amount of milk for the consistency you like.

VARIATION TIP: Change up the variety of ingredients to have this breakfast a few times a week without repeating flavors. Try raspberries and blueberries with cashews, sunflower seeds, and chia seeds, or any combination of berries, nuts, and seeds.

PER SERVING: Calories: 352; Total fat: 27g; Saturated fat: 3g; Sodium: 47mg; Carbohydrates: 21g; Fiber: 9g; Sugar: 9g; Protein: 13g

FIGS AND TOFU YOGURT WITH FLAXSEED

GLUTEN-FREE, QUICK

SERVES 4
PREP TIME: 10 minutes

14 ounces of tofu,
  silken or soft
1 banana
¼ cup unsweetened
  nondairy milk
¼ cup freshly squeezed
  lemon juice
½ cup maple
  syrup, divided
4 tablespoons ground
  flaxseed
12 figs, thinly sliced

This speedy breakfast puts the focus on two classic Mediterranean ingredients—fresh figs and yogurt. We're going to take the plant-based approach by making our own tofu-based yogurt and increase the nutrition of this meal by sprinkling in some ground flaxseed for a healthy dose of omega-3 fatty acids.

1. To make the yogurt: In a blender, mix the tofu, banana, milk, lemon juice, and ¼ cup of maple syrup until smooth.

2. Divide the yogurt between 4 bowls. Add 1 tablespoon flaxseed to each bowl and mix.

3. Evenly top each bowl with the fig slices. To finish, drizzle each bowl with the remaining ¼ cup of maple syrup on top.

VARIATION TIP: If you'd rather use regular yogurt, opt for one that contains minimal added sugars and at least 7 grams of protein per serving. Try coconut, cashew, almond, or soy-based yogurt.

PER SERVING: Calories: 332; Total fat: 6g; Saturated fat: <1g; Sodium: 23mg; Carbohydrates: 68g; Fiber: 7g; Sugar: 54g; Protein: 8g

SPINACH-TOMATO TOSTADA

SERVES 1
PREP TIME: 10 minutes

1 teaspoon extra-virgin
   olive oil, divided
1 large whole-grain tortilla
2 tablespoons diced
   red onion
¼ cup cherry
   tomatoes, halved
1 cup torn spinach
¼ cup Hummus (page 122)

PER SERVING: Calories: 373;
Total fat: 15g; Saturated
fat: 3g; Sodium: 527mg;
Carbohydrates: 44g; Fiber:
7g; Sugar: 3g; Protein: 11g

Savory dishes are sometimes the most satisfying way to start the day. For this delicious recipe, you can change out the hummus for mashed white navy beans or black turtle beans, and sprinkle 2 tablespoons of hemp hearts on top for some extra protein and variety. Be creative—the sky's the limit.

1. Preheat a large nonstick skillet over medium heat.

2. Using ½ teaspoon of olive oil, brush both sides of the tortilla.

3. In the skillet, toast the tortilla until crispy on one side, then flip the tortilla and toast the other side. Remove from the pan.

4. Add the remaining ½ teaspoon of olive oil to the skillet and sauté the onion and cherry tomatoes for 3 to 4 minutes, until the onion is translucent and fragrant.

5. Add the spinach and sauté for about 1 minute, until wilted.

6. Spread the hummus on the toasted tortilla and then top with the sautéed vegetables.

INGREDIENT TIP: Tortillas can be made with wheat, corn, seeds, or alternative grain flours. Always be sure that your wheat-based tortilla is made from whole grains for optimal health benefits. Use a corn tortilla to keep this recipe gluten-free.

VARIATION TIP: Try flavors from around the Mediterranean by using pesto in place of the hummus, or top your tortilla with olives, cucumbers, and feta cheese.

KALE AND RED PEPPER FRITTATA

GLUTEN-FREE

SERVES 4
PREP TIME: 10 minutes
COOK TIME: 20 minutes

8 eggs
½ cup unsweetened
   nondairy milk
½ teaspoon sea salt
½ teaspoon freshly
   ground black pepper
1 tablespoon extra-virgin
   olive oil
2 cups kale
   leaves, chopped
1 red bell pepper, seeded
   and chopped
1 cup cherry
   tomatoes, halved

PER SERVING: Calories: 190;
Total fat: 13g; Saturated
fat: 3g; Sodium: 432mg;
Carbohydrates: 5g; Fiber: 2g;
Sugar: 3g; Protein: 12g

The frittata is a traditional Italian egg-based dish, which is usually cooked in a skillet to brown the bottom, and then finished in the oven. If you don't own an oven-safe skillet, you can transfer the mixture to a baking dish after sautéing the vegetables and add 10 minutes to the baking time.

1. Preheat the oven to 400°F.

2. In a large mixing bowl, whisk together the eggs, milk, salt, and pepper. Set aside.

3. In an oven-safe skillet or a deep sauté pan over medium heat, heat the olive oil. Add the kale, bell pepper, and tomatoes. Cook for about 5 minutes, or until the kale is wilted and bright green.

4. Pour the whisked egg mixture into the skillet and let the eggs begin to set for 30 seconds before gently stirring with a spatula to evenly distribute the vegetables in the eggs.

5. Transfer the skillet to the oven and bake for 12 to 15 minutes, or until the eggs have set.

6. Remove the pan from the oven and let sit for 5 minutes before serving.

VARIATION TIP: This meal can be made egg-free by swapping out the eggs for chickpea flour. To make the equivalent of 1 egg, mix ¼ cup chickpea flour with ¼ cup water. A pinch of black salt adds a slight eggy flavor.

LEFTOVERS TIP: This recipe will keep in the refrigerator for about 3 days. Crumble the leftovers and put them into a whole-grain tortilla wrap or pita for a quick, healthy breakfast, lunch, or snack.

TOFU SHAKSHUKA

SERVES 4
PREP TIME: 5 minutes
COOK TIME: 25 minutes

14 ounces extra-firm
   tofu, divided
¼ cup water
1 red bell pepper, seeded
   and chopped
2 teaspoons
   ground paprika
1 teaspoon ground cumin
1 teaspoon ground
   coriander
2½ cups canned, diced
   fire-roasted tomatoes
¾ cup finely chopped
   fresh parsley, divided
1 avocado, peeled,
   seeded, and sliced

Shakshuka, which originated from North Africa, traditionally contains gently poached eggs. For this plant-based version, we're going to use tofu instead of eggs. Made from blended and pressed soybeans, tofu is an incredibly versatile, protein-packed food that has the ability to take on the flavors it's cooked in. Coriander, cumin, and paprika will impart the spicy warmth this meal is known for. Enjoy it with a piece of whole-grain bread to soak up the tomato sauce.

1. Preheat the oven to 375°F.

2. Remove the tofu from the package and wrap in a clean cloth or paper towel. Place the tofu on a plate and add a second plate on top. Apply a few heavy cans to the top plate and leave the tofu to "press" for 5 minutes.

3. Evenly slice ¾ of the tofu. Crumble the remaining quarter and set both aside, separately.

4. In an oven-safe skillet with a lid over medium-high heat, sauté the bell pepper for 3 to 4 minutes, until slightly tender.

5. Add the paprika, cumin, and coriander and stir for 1 minute. Stir in the tomatoes and ½ cup of parsley.

6. Place the tofu slices on top, cover the pan with the lid, and simmer for 10 minutes.

7. Remove the lid and transfer the pan to the oven. Bake, uncovered, for about 10 minutes, or until the tofu is crisp.

8. Top with the crumbled tofu, remaining ¼ cup parsley, and sliced avocado.

9. Divide between 4 bowls and enjoy.

VARIATION TIP: Feel free to add a few handfuls of your favorite dark leafy greens at step 4.

PER SERVING: Calories: 205; Total fat: 10g; Saturated fat: 1g; Sodium: 393mg; Carbohydrates: 16g; Fiber: 7g; Sugar: 6g; Protein: 12g

EGGS "ROTOS"

SERVES 4
PREP TIME: 15 minutes
COOK TIME: 25 minutes

4 medium Yukon Gold
  potatoes, cut into
  ¼-inch-thick rounds
¼ cup extra-virgin olive
  oil, divided
Sea salt
Freshly ground
  black pepper
1 yellow onion, sliced
2 garlic cloves, minced
4 eggs
1 teaspoon
  ground paprika
¼ cup chopped fresh
  parsley
2 teaspoons freshly
  squeezed lemon juice

PER SERVING: Calories: 325;
Total fat: 18g; Saturated
fat: 3g; Sodium: 69mg;
Carbohydrates: 31g; Fiber:
3g; Sugar: 5g; Protein: 9g

The name of this Spanish-inspired egg dish translates roughly to "broken eggs," and it's usually served on fried potatoes.

1. Preheat the oven to 375°F.

2. In a large bowl, toss the potatoes with 3 tablespoons of olive oil. Season with salt and pepper to taste.

3. In a baking dish, layer the potatoes.

4. Bake the potatoes in the oven for 14 minutes, flipping them halfway through.

5. In a large skillet, heat the remaining 1 tablespoon of olive oil and sauté the onion and garlic for about 2 minutes, until the onion is translucent. Remove the mixture and set aside.

6. Carefully crack the eggs into the same pan and cook for 2 to 3 minutes, until the whites begin to set. Flip the eggs and cook for an additional 30 to 60 seconds.

7. Divide the potatoes evenly between 4 plates and add the sautéed vegetables on top. Slide a cooked egg on top of the potatoes and vegetables and garnish each plate with ¼ teaspoon paprika, 3 teaspoons parsley, and ½ teaspoon lemon juice.

VARIATION TIP: To satisfy a bigger appetite, use 2 eggs per person instead of 1, or consider adding some tofu "chorizo" (see page 46).

TOFU SCRAMBLE

GLUTEN-FREE

SERVES 4
PREP TIME: 10 minutes
COOK TIME: 10 minutes

14 ounces extra-firm tofu
1 tablespoon extra-virgin
   olive oil
1 white onion, diced
2 garlic cloves, minced
1 red bell pepper, seeded
   and chopped
1 orange bell pepper,
   seeded and chopped
2 cups chopped baby
   spinach
¼ cup nutritional yeast
1 teaspoon turmeric
Sea salt
Freshly ground
   black pepper
¼ teaspoon black salt
   (optional)

PER SERVING: Calories:
188; Total fat: 9g; Saturated
fat: 1g; Sodium: 24mg;
Carbohydrates: 13g; Fiber:
5g; Sugar: 4g; Protein: 15g

Let's scramble the typical take on eggs with a plant-based alternative. Tofu, with the right seasoning, can have a taste and texture very similar to scrambled eggs, but has the added health benefits of being lower in cholesterol and higher in calcium.

1. Remove the tofu from the package and wrap in a clean cloth or paper towels. Place the tofu on a plate and add a second plate on top. Apply a few heavy cans to the top plate and leave the tofu to "press" for 5 minutes.

2. Unwrap the tofu and mash in a large bowl with the back of a fork until it's broken into small chunks—like scrambled eggs.

3. In a large nonstick skillet, heat the olive oil. Add the onion, garlic, and red and orange bell peppers and sauté for 4 to 5 minutes, until the onion is translucent.

4. Add the tofu, spinach, nutritional yeast, and turmeric. Cook, stirring, until the spinach is wilted and the tofu is heated through.

5. Season with sea salt, black pepper, and the black salt (if using). Divide between 4 plates and serve.

VARIATION TIP: Add tomatoes, chopped asparagus, mushrooms, and even olives for variety to this easy breakfast.

LEFTOVERS TIP: Eat this for any meal of the day as is or as a side. I love to throw this on top of sweet potato hash with sautéed onions and mushrooms. You can combine this with just about anything you would add to scrambled eggs.

ONE-PAN TOFU "CHORIZO" AND SQUASH BREAKFAST HASH

GLUTEN-FREE

SERVES 4
PREP TIME: 10 minutes
COOK TIME: 20 minutes

3 tablespoons extra-virgin olive oil, divided, plus more for greasing the baking sheet

14 ounces extra-firm tofu, crumbled

2 tablespoons soy sauce

1 tablespoon apple cider vinegar

1 tablespoon chili powder

2 teaspoons paprika

1 teaspoon garlic powder

1 teaspoon oregano

¼ teaspoon cumin

¼ teaspoon ground cloves

2 cups butternut squash, peeled and chopped into small cubes

½ cup chopped cilantro

2 avocados, seeded, peeled, and sliced

There's nothing better than a one-pan breakfast that's done in 30 minutes. Chorizo is a type of pork sausage, but here we'll be making it with tofu for a plant-based alternative. Squash is high in vitamin A, which is crucial for protecting our vision, skin, immune system, and reproductive system, and vitamin C, which, when eaten with foods high in iron, like tofu, can help improve the absorption of iron, decreasing the likelihood of diet-related anemia.

1. Preheat the oven to 350°F. Lightly grease a rimmed baking sheet with olive oil.

2. Remove the tofu from the package and wrap in a clean cloth or paper towels. Place the tofu on a plate and add a second plate on top. Weigh down the top plate with a few heavy cans and leave the tofu to "press" for 5 minutes.

3. In a small bowl, mix 2 tablespoons of oil, the soy sauce, vinegar, chili powder, paprika, garlic powder, oregano, cumin, and cloves.

4. In a large bowl, crumble the tofu block with your fingers or a fork. Evenly coat the tofu crumbles with the spice mixture.

5. Spread the "chorizo" crumbles evenly on the prepared baking sheet.

6. In another bowl, toss the squash with the remaining 1 tablespoon of olive oil.

7. Add the squash to the baking sheet with the tofu, place in the oven, and bake for about 25 minutes, stirring halfway through the cooking time, until the tofu is chewy and the squash is cooked through.

8. Divide evenly between 4 plates and garnish with the cilantro and avocado.

INGREDIENT TIP: Frozen butternut squash is a good option, as it will already be peeled and parboiled before being frozen. This reduces the prep time and helps avoid the need to buy an entire squash for one meal.

VARIATION TIP: Leave out the squash if you'd like to make just the "chorizo," and add it to other dishes, such as the Pumpkin Mac 'n' Cheese (page 83).

PER SERVING: Calories: 370; Total fat: 27g; Saturated fat: 4g; Sodium: 514mg; Carbohydrates: 23g; Fiber: 11g; Sugar: 3g; Protein: 14g

Charred
Kale Salad,
page **53**

SALADS AND SOUPS

MIXED BEAN SALAD

SERVES 3
PREP TIME: 10 minutes

1 (16-ounce) can mixed
  beans, drained
  and rinsed
2 cups cherry
  tomatoes, halved
1 cup fresh parsley,
  finely chopped
1 tablespoon
  Italian seasoning
  (ingredients follow)
1 tablespoon apple
  cider vinegar
1 tablespoon maple syrup
1 tablespoon extra-virgin
  olive oil
Sea salt
Freshly ground
  black pepper

FOR THE ITALIAN SEASONING

1½ teaspoons oregano
1 teaspoon marjoram
1 teaspoon thyme
½ teaspoon basil
½ teaspoon rosemary
½ teaspoon sage

This satisfying bean salad is a simple way to add more plant-based protein into your day. It features the Mediterranean flavors of parsley, basil, oregano, and thyme. You can eat this as a meal on its own or throw it on a bed of salad greens for an extra serving of vegetables.

1. In a large bowl, combine the beans, cherry tomatoes, parsley, Italian seasoning, vinegar, maple syrup, and olive oil.

2. Season with salt and pepper, to taste.

INGREDIENT TIP: If you can't find a can of mixed beans, feel free to use any combination of beans you like. I suggest trying chickpeas, white cannellini beans, black turtle beans, pinto beans, and red kidney beans. One 16-ounce can of mixed beans holds approximately 2 cups of beans. Make a large batch of the Italian seasoning, and store in an airtight jar for future use. Also, feel free to be creative with the spices if you don't have all the ingredients for the Italian seasoning.

LEFTOVERS TIP: This salad becomes extra-flavorful after marinating for a day in the refrigerator, and it stores up to 5 days, making it an excellent premade lunch option.

VARIATION TIP: Top with olives, avocado, mixed greens, or diced cucumber.

PER SERVING: Calories: 228; Total fat: 5g; Saturated fat: 5g; Sodium: 20mg; Carbohydrates: 37g; Fiber: 13g; Sugar: 6g; Protein: 10g

TZATZIKI PASTA SALAD

SERVES 4

PREP TIME: 10 minutes, plus 30 minutes to soak cashews

COOK TIME: 15 minutes

½ cup raw cashews

4 ounces whole-grain pasta

1 tablespoon unsweetened nondairy milk

1 tablespoon extra-virgin olive oil

1 tablespoon freshly squeezed lemon juice

¼ cucumber, seeded and diced

1 garlic clove

1 tablespoon fresh dill

1 teaspoon sea salt

¼ teaspoon freshly ground black pepper

¼ cup kalamata olives

¼ cup black olives, pitted

¼ cup sun-dried tomatoes

¼ cup artichoke hearts, chopped

For a taste of Greece, try this healthy spin on a pasta salad that doesn't rely on a dairy-based sauce. Cashews, which have a mild flavor and are high in iron, copper, vitamin K, and magnesium, make an amazing creamy base for dressings and sauces.

1. In a small bowl, soak the cashews in boiling water for 30 minutes, then drain and rinse.

2. Cook the pasta according to the package directions.

3. Prepare the tzatziki while the pasta cooks. In a blender or food processor, blend the cashews, milk, olive oil, lemon juice, cucumber, garlic, dill, salt, and pepper. You may have to scrape down the sides of the blender a few times to ensure the sauce is really smooth.

4. Remove the pasta from the stove when al dente, drain, and rinse with cool water.

5. In a large mixing bowl, combine the pasta, kalamata olives, black olives, tomatoes, and artichoke hearts.

6. Add the tzatziki and mix well to combine.

PREP TIP: If you use an English cucumber, there's no need to seed it before dicing.

VARIATION TIP: For more protein, add 2 cups of cooked, drained, and rinsed beans of your choice. For more veggies, add 4 cups of mixed baby greens.

PER SERVING: Calories: 264; Total fat: 14g; Saturated fat: 2g; Sodium: 861mg; Carbohydrates: 31g; Fiber: 5g; Sugar: 3g; Protein: 8g

CRANBERRY, BROCCOLI, AND QUINOA SALAD

GLUTEN-FREE

SERVES 4

PREP TIME: 10 minutes, plus 30 minutes to refrigerate

COOK TIME: 15 minutes

⅓ cup uncooked quinoa, rinsed and drained

1 cup water

2⅔ cups fresh broccoli florets, chopped

2 scallions, both white and green parts, diced

¼ cup pumpkin seeds, raw, shelled, and unsalted

¾ cup unsweetened dried cranberries,

3 tablespoons extra-virgin olive oil

2 tablespoons apple cider vinegar

2 teaspoons Dijon mustard

3 tablespoons freshly squeezed orange juice

Sea salt

Freshly ground black pepper

PER SERVING: Calories: 316; Total fat: 15g; Saturated fat: 2g; Sodium: 114mg; Carbohydrates: 40g; Fiber: 4g; Sugar: 26g; Protein: 6g

Quinoa, considered to be an "ancient grain," is actually a seed and has a soft nutty flavor when cooked. An easy substitute for rice in most recipes, it has a complete amino-acid protein profile, similar to those found in animal-based proteins. The fruit in this recipe adds a sweet, tart element for some extra zing.

1. In a medium saucepan with a lid, combine the quinoa and water and bring to a boil over high heat. Reduce the heat, cover with the lid, and simmer for 12 to 15 minutes, or until the water is absorbed. Remove the lid and fluff with a fork. Set aside.

2. While the quinoa cools, in a medium mixing bowl, combine the broccoli, scallions, pumpkin seeds, and cranberries.

3. In a small bowl, make the dressing by whisking together the olive oil, vinegar, mustard, and orange juice. Season with salt and pepper to taste.

4. Add the quinoa to the broccoli mix and drizzle with the dressing. Toss the salad well.

5. Refrigerate for 30 minutes before serving.

VARIATION TIP: Cook the quinoa in Vegetable Broth (page 123) instead of water for some extra flavor. Try a combination of shredded Brussels sprouts and arugula leaves in addition to the broccoli, or sprinkle some fresh pomegranate seeds on top, and get creative with different nuts and seeds, such as sunflower seeds, pecans, or almonds.

CHARRED KALE SALAD

GLUTEN-FREE

SERVES 4
PREP TIME: 10 minutes
COOK TIME: 10 minutes

2 tablespoons toasted
   sesame seeds
1 tablespoon extra-virgin
   olive oil
8 cups kale leaves,
   stems removed and
   roughly torn
¼ cup pumpkin seeds,
   raw, shelled, and
   unsalted
1 orange, peeled and cut
   into segments
1 grapefruit, peeled and
   cut into segments
1 cup Tahini Dressing
   (page 131)

PER SERVING: Calories: 372;
Total fat: 32g; Saturated
fat: 5g; Sodium: 45mg;
Carbohydrates: 19g; Fiber:
6g; Sugar: 9g; Protein: 8g

Kale, a dark, leafy, cruciferous green, ranks as one of the most nutrient-dense foods. It's loaded with calcium, vitamin K, manganese, and other important minerals for optimal health. Despite kale's standout nutrition profile, its tough leaves can be difficult to eat without thoroughly massaging each leaf to deconstruct the fiber. To skip that tedious step, char it for tender, delicious kale within just a few minutes.

1. If your sesame seeds aren't already toasted, place them in a dry medium skillet over medium heat and toast them gently for 2 to 3 minutes, or until they begin to brown slightly and become fragrant. Remove them from the pan.

2. In the same pan, heat the olive oil over medium heat. Add 4 cups of kale and cook undisturbed for about 1 minute, then lightly toss and cook for about 1 minute more, charring it slightly.

3. Remove the kale from the pan to a serving plate and set aside. Repeat the process with the remaining 2 cups of kale, adding it to the plate.

4. Top the charred kale with the toasted sesame seeds, pumpkin seeds, orange segments, and grapefruit segments.

5. Drizzle the Tahini Dressing over the salad and serve.

VARIATION TIP: Add some cooked whole-grain pasta, farro, quinoa, or couscous to add complex carbohydrates for a more filling meal.

CUCUMBER, TOMATO, AND CHICKPEA SALAD

GLUTEN-FREE, QUICK

SERVES 4
PREP TIME: 5 to
10 minutes

1 cup whole-grain
   couscous
2 English
   cucumbers, diced
2 cups cherry
   tomatoes, halved
2 (16-ounce) cans
   chickpeas, drained
   and rinsed
½ cup Sumac Dressing
   (page 132)

With the quick-cooking convenience of couscous, this time-saving recipe comes together with little effort. My favorite way to make oil-and-vinegar–based salad dressings is to put all the ingredients into a small mason jar, put the lid on, and shake it silly. It's always a hit with the kids and a great way to get others in your house involved.

1. Cook the couscous according to the package directions. Allow to cool while you make the rest of the salad.

2. In a large bowl, combine the cucumbers, cherry tomatoes, and chickpeas.

3. Add the couscous to the cucumber mix, drizzle with the dressing, and stir well.

VARIATION TIP: No couscous on hand? Swap it for farro, spelt, or quinoa.

LEFTOVERS TIP: This salad will store well in the refrigerator for 3 to 5 days and the flavors will improve after a day or two of marinating.

PER SERVING: Calories: 551; Total fat: 19g; Saturated fat: 2g; Sodium: 968mg; Carbohydrates: 82g; Fiber: 15g; Sugar: 22g; Protein: 18g

ZUCCHINI NOODLES WITH TOMATOES AND PESTO

GLUTEN-FREE, QUICK

SERVES 2
PREP TIME: 10 minutes

2 medium zucchini
2 cups cherry
   tomatoes, halved
1 batch Perfect Pesto
   (page 128)

This recipe is a tasty way to plate vegetables. Zucchini makes an easy replacement for grain-based pasta and adds a few extra servings of vegetables with little effort. The noodles can be enjoyed either warm or cold, and can be prepared ahead of time for a grab-and-go lunch.

1. Using a spiralizer or a vegetable peeler, make noodles out of the zucchini.

2. In a large bowl, combine the zucchini noodles with the tomatoes and the pesto.

INGREDIENT TIP: You can make vegetable noodles out of carrots, sweet potatoes, cucumbers, beets, parsnips, rutabaga, and turnips. Be sure to toss any root veggies into a pan for a quick sauté before eating them.

VARIATION TIP: For more protein, add 1 cup cooked white navy beans to the dish.

LEFTOVERS TIP: Store leftovers in an airtight container in the refrigerator for 1 to 2 days.

PER SERVING: Calories: 511; Total fat: 43g; Saturated fat: 5g; Sodium: 32mg; Carbohydrates: 22g; Fiber: 8g; Sugar: 8g; Protein: 16g

TOMATO BISQUE

GLUTEN-FREE, QUICK

SERVES 4
PREP TIME: 5 minutes
COOK TIME: 15 minutes

1 tablespoon extra-virgin
    olive oil
½ cup diced celery
½ yellow onion, diced
2 garlic cloves, minced
1 (28-ounce) can plum
    tomatoes, whole
    or diced
2 cups Vegetable Broth
    (page 123)
1 (16-ounce) can white
    cannellini beans,
    drained and rinsed
1 tablespoon white miso
    paste (optional)
½ cup chopped basil
    leaves, divided
½ cup nutritional yeast
Sea salt
Freshly ground
    black pepper

Originating from France, bisque is a smooth, creamy tomato-based soup that's typically made with seafood broth. This plant-based variation is packed with protein for a filling meal that you can pair with your favorite crusty bread.

1. In a medium saucepan with a lid over medium heat, heat the olive oil. Add the celery, onion, and garlic and sauté until fragrant, 3 to 4 minutes.

2. Add the tomatoes, broth, beans, and miso paste (if using) and simmer for 10 minutes with the lid on but cracked open. Remove from the heat and add ¼ cup of basil.

3. Use an immersion blender, or transfer the soup in batches to a blender, and blend until smooth

4. Stir in the nutritional yeast and remaining ¼ cup of basil. Season with salt and pepper to taste and serve.

INGREDIENT TIP: Miso paste is a fermented soy paste that adds an umami flavor to the soup, deepening the flavor without adding seafood or cheese.

VARIATION TIP: Use chickpeas, silken tofu, soaked cashews, or cooked white navy beans for a protein source if you don't have cannellini beans on hand.

LEFTOVERS TIP: Store in the refrigerator for up to 5 days or in the freezer for up to 1 month.

PER SERVING: Calories: 248; Total fat: 5g; Saturated fat: 1g; Sodium: 634mg; Carbohydrates: 35g; Fiber: 12g; Sugar: 8g; Protein: 16g

SPLIT PEA SOUP

SERVES 4
PREP TIME: 5 minutes
COOK TIME: 20 minutes

2 tablespoons extra-virgin
   olive oil
1 large white onion,
   finely diced
2 garlic cloves, minced
1 teaspoon sea salt
4 cups Vegetable Broth
   (page 123)
2 cups dried green
   (or yellow) split
   peas, rinsed
1 cup unsweetened
   nondairy milk
1 tablespoon freshly
   squeezed lemon juice
Smoked paprika,
   for garnish
Red chili flakes, for
   garnish

Split pea soup was a pantry staple for my family when I was a kid, but after moving to a plant-based diet, it was difficult to find ham-free versions. Fortunately, this fresh, plant-based recipe lives up to my childhood memories, and more.

1. In a large saucepan with a lid over medium heat, heat the oil. Add the onion and garlic and cook until soft and translucent, about 3 minutes.

2. Add the salt, broth, and split peas to the saucepan and simmer, with the lid on, for about 15 minutes, or until the peas are cooked through, but not mushy.

3. In a blender, combine half the soup, the milk, and the lemon juice and blend until smooth. Transfer the soup back to the pot and stir well.

4. Serve garnished with paprika and red chili flakes.

VARIATION TIP: Serve with freshly chopped mint, a dollop of Tzatziki (page 130), or unsweetened tofu yogurt (see page 39).

LEFTOVERS TIP: Store in the refrigerator for up to 5 days or in the freezer for up to 2 months.

PER SERVING: Calories: 423; Total fat: 9g; Saturated fat: 1g; Sodium: 1225mg; Carbohydrates: 56g; Fiber: 9g; Sugar: 6g; Protein: 25g

EGYPTIAN-INSPIRED LENTIL SOUP

GLUTEN-FREE

SERVES 4
PREP TIME: 10 minutes
COOK TIME: 20 minutes

3¼ cups water
1 cup dried red
   lentils, rinsed
1¼ yellow onions, thinly
   sliced, divided
2 garlic cloves, minced
½ teaspoon cumin
½ teaspoon sea salt
2 tablespoons freshly
   squeezed lemon juice

Cumin adds a vibrant touch to this hearty soup. The red lentils deliver plant-based protein and iron, while nutrient-dense onions help promote overall health through antioxidants, cancer-fighting compounds, and antibacterial properties.

1. In a large pot over high heat, bring the water to a boil.

2. Add the lentils, two-thirds of the onions, and the the garlic, cumin, and salt. Lower the heat and simmer for 20 minutes.

3. In a separate skillet, over medium-high heat, caramelize the remaining onions with a splash of water. Stir frequently and add more water when needed to keep the onions from sticking to the pan. Cook until soft and brown, about 15 minutes.

4. Add the lemon juice to the soup and use an immersion blender to blend the soup until smooth.

5. Divide the soup between 4 bowls and top with the caramelized onions.

VARIATION TIP: Serve with freshly chopped cilantro, a dollop of coconut yogurt, or crushed red pepper flakes.

LEFTOVERS TIP: Store in the refrigerator for up to 1 week or in the freezer for up to 2 months.

PER SERVING: Calories: 189; Total fat: 1g; Saturated fat: 0g; Sodium: 299mg; Carbohydrates: 32g; Fiber: 8g; Sugar: 3g; Protein: 14g

MINESTRONE

SERVES 4
PREP TIME: 10 minutes
COOK TIME: 35 minutes

1 teaspoon extra-virgin
   olive oil
1 yellow onion,
   finely chopped
1 carrot, peeled
   and chopped
4 garlic cloves, minced
1 tablespoon Italian
   seasoning (page 50)
1 teaspoon sea salt
¼ cup canned
   tomato paste
3½ cups canned diced
   tomatoes
4 cups Vegetable Broth
   (page 123)
2 cups kidney beans,
   drained and rinsed
1 cup frozen green
   beans, chopped
1½ cups dried
   whole-grain or
   gluten-free pasta

Rich in vegetables, minestrone originates from Italy, where it's made up of varying ingredients depending on the season and the region. It's not unheard of to prepare this soup with winter squash or cabbage, or to top it with pesto. Don't worry if you don't have all the ingredients on hand for this recipe—just use what you have.

1. In a large pot over medium heat, heat the oil. Add the onion and cook for 3 to 5 minutes or until softened. Add the carrot, garlic, Italian seasoning, and salt and stir to combine. Cook for 2 to 3 minutes more. Stir in the tomato paste and continue to cook for 1 minute.

2. Add the diced tomatoes, vegetable broth, and kidney beans and stir until combined.

3. Add the green beans. Bring to a gentle boil and continue to cook for about 25 minutes, or until the vegetables are tender. Season with additional salt if needed.

4. Meanwhile, cook the pasta according to the package directions. Drain, rinse well, and set aside.

5. To serve, divide the soup between 4 bowls and stir in the cooked pasta.

LEFTOVERS TIP: Keep in the refrigerator for up to 4 days in an airtight container, or store in the freezer for up to 3 months.

PER SERVING: Calories: 330; Total fat: 3g; Saturated fat: 1g; Sodium: 1694mg; Carbohydrates: 64g; Fiber: 13g; Sugar: 16g; Protein: 14g

Creamy Avocado-Chickpea Salad Sandwich, page **64**

CHAPTER 5

WRAPS AND SANDWICHES

GRILLED EGGPLANT SANDWICH

SERVES 4
PREP TIME: 10 minutes
COOK TIME: 20 minutes

1 small eggplant, cut into ¼-inch-thick slices
Portobello mushrooms, cut into ¼-inch-thick slices (1 cup)
1 red bell pepper, cut into ¼-inch-thick slices
½ red onion, cut into ¼-inch-thick slices
2 garlic cloves, minced
1 tablespoon Italian seasoning (page 50)
2 tablespoons extra-virgin olive oil
4 whole-grain ciabatta buns
¾ cup tomato sauce

PER SERVING: Calories: 280; Total fat: 10g; Saturated fat: 2g; Sodium: 464mg; Carbohydrates: 41g; Fiber: 9g; Sugar: 10g; Protein: 9g

This sandwich is worth the effort. If you have a grill, I strongly encourage you to use it for the eggplant, as it will provide a beautifully rich texture and taste, but you can also use the oven to roast the eggplant and other vegetables. Eggplant is a part of the nightshade plant family, meaning that it shares similar nutrients and characteristics of tomatoes and peppers. That's probably why these ingredients go so well together.

1. Preheat the grill to medium-high heat or preheat the oven to 425°F.

2. In a large bowl, toss together the eggplant, mushrooms, bell pepper, onion, garlic, Italian seasoning, and olive oil until well combined.

3. Grill the vegetables on medium-high heat for 7 to 8 minutes, flipping the eggplant halfway through, until grill marks form and the eggplant is cooked. If using the oven, roast the vegetables for about 20 minutes, flipping the eggplant halfway through, until the eggplant is cooked.

4. Cut open the ciabatta buns and spread the tomato sauce on the inside of both halves of each bun.

5. Top the lower half of the bun with ¼ of the grilled vegetables, add any additional toppings of your choosing, and put the top half of the bun on to close the sandwich.

VARIATION TIP: You can add other vegetables like zucchini or tomato or add extra protein with grilled tofu or chicken. Toppings to try: Tzatziki (page 130), Hummus (page 122), Perfect Pesto (page 128), and Soft "Cheese" Spread (page 127).

LENTIL SHAWARMA LETTUCE WRAP

GLUTEN-FREE, QUICK

SERVES 4
PREP TIME: 5 minutes
COOK TIME: 5 minutes

1 tablespoon freshly
   squeezed lemon juice
1 tablespoon tomato
   paste or sauce
2 tablespoons
   low-sodium soy sauce
1 (16-ounce) can brown
   lentils, drained
   and rinsed
2 teaspoons
   ground cumin
1 teaspoon ground
   coriander
1 teaspoon paprika
¼ teaspoon ground
   cinnamon
¼ teaspoon
   ground cloves
4 large romaine
   lettuce leaves
½ cup diced cucumber
½ cup diced tomatoes
4 tablespoons
   kalamata olives
½ cup Tzatziki (page 130)

Traditional shawarma is a Mediterranean café staple made from spiced meat that's grilled on a rotating spit. This healthier, plant-based version enhances the filling lentils with aromatic seasonings.

1. In a medium bowl, stir together the lemon juice, tomato paste, and soy sauce until well combined.

2. Add the lentils, cumin, coriander, paprika, cinnamon, and cloves and stir until the lentils are evenly coated.

3. In a medium skillet, gently warm the lentil mixture over medium heat for about 5 minutes, or until thoroughly warmed through.

4. Add ¼ of the lentil mixture to each of the 4 large romaine lettuce leaves.

5. Top each lettuce wrap with the cucumber, tomatoes, and olives, then drizzle the Tzatziki over the filling before rolling the lettuce leaf.

VARIATION TIP: Try adding 1 cup of oyster mushrooms to step 1 to cook with the lentils and spices. Once the mushrooms are softened and juicy, shred them with two forks to bring a meaty texture to your sandwich.

PER SERVING: Calories: 193; Total fat: 5g; Saturated fat: 1g; Sodium: 534mg; Carbohydrates: 28g; Fiber: 10g; Sugar: 4g; Protein: 13g

CREAMY AVOCADO-CHICKPEA SALAD SANDWICH

SERVES 3
PREP TIME: 15 minutes

1 (16-ounce) can
 chickpeas, drained
 and rinsed
1 avocado
2 teaspoons apple
 cider vinegar
1 garlic clove, minced
2 tablespoons
 dried parsley
Sea salt
Freshly ground
 black pepper
6 slices whole-grain bread
1 cup baby spinach
½ cucumber, cut into
 ¼-inch-thick rounds

PER SERVING: Calories: 436;
Total fat: 13g; Saturated
fat: 2g; Sodium: 412mg;
Carbohydrates: 64g; Fiber:
15g; Sugar: 8g; Protein: 19g

I love this sandwich as a plant-based alternative to egg salad sandwiches. The mashed chickpeas have a similar texture, while the avocado and apple cider vinegar provide a creamy and tangy taste similar to mayonnaise. You can enjoy it as is, with a light soup, or served with a plate full of chopped raw vegetables. Make it gluten-free by using gluten-free bread or a lettuce wrap.

1. In a medium bowl, mash the chickpeas and avocado together with the back of a fork.

2. Add the vinegar, garlic, and parsley to the chickpea mash and stir well. Season with salt and pepper to taste.

3. Spread the chickpea mash on 3 slices of bread.

4. Top each with ⅓ of the spinach and cucumber.

5. Close the sandwiches with the other 3 slices of bread and enjoy.

VARIATION TIP: Fresh dill makes a delicious addition to this sandwich. Also consider mixing 1 teaspoon miso paste into the chickpea mash for greater depth of flavor, or 2 tablespoons finely diced white or red onion, which can give this sandwich a little kick.

LEFTOVERS TIP: Store leftover avocado-chickpea mash in the refrigerator in an airtight container for up to 2 days. Leftovers can also be repurposed by throwing some onto a large bowl of mixed greens for a salad with some healthy protein and fats.

FALAFEL-STUFFED PITA

SERVES 3
PREP TIME: 10 minutes
COOK TIME: 20 minutes

2 (16-ounce) cans
  chickpeas, drained,
  rinsed, and patted dry
8 garlic cloves
¾ cup fresh parsley
1 tablespoon cumin
½ teaspoon sea salt
4 tablespoons
  all-purpose
  whole-grain flour
3 whole-grain pitas
1 cucumber, cut into
  ¼-inch-thick rounds
2 Roma tomatoes, cut into
  ¼-inch-thick slices
⅓ cup Tahini Dressing
  (page 131) or Tzatziki
  (page 130)

PER SERVING: Calories: 563;
Total fat: 16g; Saturated
fat: 2g; Sodium: 1034mg;
Carbohydrates: 90g; Fiber:
19g; Sugar: 11g; Protein: 23g

Falafel is traditionally made by deep-frying balls of blended, soaked, raw chickpeas, herbs, and spices. This hands-off way of making falafel by baking it in the oven makes for a healthier, easier dish.

1. Preheat the oven to 375°F. Line a rimmed baking sheet with parchment paper. Set aside.

2. In a food processor, blend together the chickpeas, garlic, parsley, cumin, and salt until the mixture is crumbly. You may have to stop and scrape the sides of the food processor a few times to ensure all of the ingredients are well incorporated.

3. Add the flour 1 tablespoon at a time until the mixture becomes a dough that can be shaped into small patties without sticking to your hands.

4. Scoop out roughly 2 tablespoons of the mixture at a time and roll into a ball, then press to form a patty. Continue with all of the dough to make roughly 12 patties.

5. Place the patties on the prepared baking sheet, and bake in the oven for about 20 minutes, until golden brown, turning them over after about 12 minutes. Remove from the oven.

6. Split open the top of the pitas and add 3 warm falafel patties to each, along with cucumber and tomato slices.

7. Drizzle your sauce of choice on top and close the pita.

MEATLESS GYROS

SERVES 4
PREP TIME: 10 minutes
COOK TIME: 13 minutes

2 cups sliced portobello
  mushrooms
⅔ cup sliced red onion
1½ tablespoons apple
  cider vinegar
1½ tablespoons
  reduce-sodium
  soy sauce
2 teaspoons
  ground cumin
1 teaspoon ground
  coriander
1 teaspoon paprika
¼ teaspoon cinnamon
¼ teaspoon
  ground cloves
3 to 4 tablespoons water
⅔ cup Tzatziki (page 130)
4 whole-grain flatbreads
2 cups chopped lettuce
⅔ cucumber, seeded
  and diced

PER SERVING: Calories:
260; Total fat: 7g; Saturated
fat: 1g; Sodium: 450mg;
Carbohydrates: 40g; Fiber:
4g; Sugar: 6g; Protein: 10g

Most of my memories of gyros, the Greek specialty
with roots in Turkey, consist of buying them off a food
cart at local carnivals and street fairs. Since going
plant-based, I've learned some simple ways to repli-
cate the flavors and textures of meat-based favorites
without the meat. While gyros are typically made from
pork, lamb, or chicken, the portobello mushrooms in
this dish offer a meaty texture while keeping you on
your plant-based plan.

1. In a medium saucepan with a lid over medium
   heat, combine the mushrooms, red onion, apple
   cider vinegar, soy sauce, cumin, coriander,
   paprika, cinnamon, and cloves.

2. Cover the pan and cook for about 5 minutes, or
   until the mushrooms are browned and the onion
   is soft.

3. Deglaze the pan with the water, stirring to scrape
   up the browned bits from the bottom, then cook,
   covered, for another 8 minutes.

4. Assemble the sandwich by spreading tzatziki on
   each flatbread, crust to crust. Layer half of each
   flatbread with the cooked mushrooms, chopped
   lettuce, and diced cucumber. Fold the flatbreads
   in half over the fillings.

VARIATION TIP: For a soy-free version, try the Sumac Dressing (page 132) instead of the Tzatziki. Add vegetables such
as green bell pepper strips, olives, and diced tomatoes for a
different flavor.

RAINBOW LETTUCE WRAP

GLUTEN-FREE, QUICK

SERVES 2
PREP TIME: 10 minutes

2 large collard
greens' leaves
¼ cup Roasted Red
Pepper and Lentil Dip
(page 111), divided
(optional)
¼ red bell pepper, cut
into thin strips
¼ yellow bell pepper, cut
into thin strips
½ carrot, peeled and cut
into sticks
½ cucumber, cut
into sticks

Using a large leafy green in place of bread is a great way to get an extra serving of vegetables, keep a sandwich gluten- or grain-free, and lighten the meal. This wrap is a refreshing option for lunch, a snack, or an accompaniment to your favorite protein. I suggest trying it with a side of the One-Pan Rosemary-Roasted Tofu (page 84) or Chicken Souvlaki (page 103).

1. Roll the collard leaves a couple of times to break the fibers a little, so they're easier to roll when assembled.

2. If using the Roasted Red Pepper and Lentil Dip, spread half on each collard leaf.

3. Lay the red and yellow bell pepper, carrot, and cucumber facing the same direction in the center of each collard leaf.

4. Fold the bottom of the leaf up and hold it in place while you fold the top of the leaf into the center of the wrap.

5. Rotate the wrap 90 degrees, so the top and bottom become the sides, and fold the bottom side of the leaf up to the center while rolling the wrap away from you to wrap the leaf tightly around itself.

VARIATION TIP: Use any large, dark leafy green you have on hand in place of the collard greens, such as rainbow Swiss chard or kale. You can also use any colorful vegetables of your choosing to layer into this wrap.

PER SERVING: Calories: 34; Total fat: <1g; Saturated fat: <1g; Sodium: 19mg; Carbohydrates: 7g; Fiber: 3g; Sugar: 3g; Protein: 2g

CARROT, HUMMUS, AND ARUGULA WRAP

QUICK

SERVES 2
PREP TIME: 10 minutes

⅔ cup Hummus (page 122)
2 whole-grain
  tortilla wraps
1 medium carrot, cut into
  matchsticks
2 cups arugula
½ teaspoon paprika

Arugula is a spicy, leafy herb that has a peppery taste. It contains more calcium and vitamin K (which are both important for healthy blood clotting) than kale. Keeping in line with the principles of the Mediterranean diet, this wrap is perfect for a grab-and-go weekday lunch.

1. Spread half the hummus evenly on each tortilla.

2. Add half the carrot sticks to each tortilla.

3. Top each tortilla with 1 cup arugula and sprinkle ¼ teaspoon paprika on top.

4. Roll the tortilla wraps tightly and cut in half.

INGREDIENT TIP: Instead of slicing the carrot, you could also grate it, shred it, spiralize it, or create ribbons with it.

VARIATION TIP: For an extra kick, sprinkle on some cayenne pepper or dried chili flakes along with the paprika.

PER SERVING: Calories: 412; Total fat: 21g; Saturated fat: 3g; Sodium: 770mg; Carbohydrates: 49; Fiber: 9g; Sugar: 6g; Protein: 12g

VEGGIE PITA PIZZA WITH HUMMUS

QUICK

SERVES 2
PREP TIME: 5 minutes
COOK TIME: 10 minutes

2 teaspoons extra-virgin
    olive oil
¼ red bell pepper, cut
    into thin strips
¼ zucchini, cut into
    thin slices
¼ cup diced mushrooms
¼ cup diced red onion
½ cup Hummus (page 122)
½ cup tomato sauce
    (optional)
2 whole wheat pitas
¼ cup nutritional yeast
    (optional)

Everyone loves eating pizza on nights when they don't feel like cooking, but the kind you grew up with comes with a lot of unhealthy consequences. Luckily, this quick plant-based version can keep you on track with your goals while still satisfying your desire for some Friday-night (or any night) comfort food.

1. Preheat the oven to 350°F.

2. In a large skillet, heat the oil and sauté the bell pepper, zucchini, mushrooms, and onion until the vegetables are tender.

3. Spread ¼ cup hummus and ¼ cup tomato sauce (if using) over each pita and top with the sautéed vegetables.

4. Heat in the oven on a rimmed baking sheet for 8 to 10 minutes. You'll want the pita to be toasted, but not burnt.

5. Sprinkle the nutritional yeast (if using) on top of each pizza for a cheesy flavor.

VARIATION TIP: Swap in other pizza toppings, such as green bell peppers, olives, broccoli florets, sun-dried tomatoes, or shredded artichokes. You can also use Perfect Pesto (page 128) in place of the tomato sauce.

PER SERVING: Calories: 376; Total fat: 19g; Saturated fat: 3g; Sodium: 618mg; Carbohydrates: 46g; Fiber: 8g; Sugar: 6g; Protein: 11g

TUNA SALAD CHARD WRAP

GLUTEN-FREE, QUICK

SERVES 2
PREP TIME: 10 minutes

½ cucumber, seeded
   and diced
2 scallions, green and
   white parts, diced
½ cup cherry
   tomatoes, halved
¼ cup diced
   kalamata olives
1 can tuna (packed in
   water), drained
¼ cup Sumac Dressing
   (page 132)
4 rainbow Swiss
   chard leaves

Tuna sandwiches are a classic, and this updated wrap will have you stocking up on canned tuna for those times when you want a satisfying lunch. The fish is high in omega-3 fatty acids, so this recipe is great for your joints, heart, brain function, and even mood.

1. In a medium bowl, mix the cucumber, scallions, cherry tomatoes, olives, and tuna.

2. Drizzle the dressing into the bowl and stir well to combine and evenly coat the tuna salad.

3. Scoop out ¼ of the salad and place on each rainbow chard leaf.

4. Roll the leaf slowly to wrap the salad within, or keep the leaf open for a tuna salad chard boat.

PREP TIP: Make the tuna salad ahead of time and store it in the refrigerator for up to 3 days for easy lunches.

VARIATION TIP: Add 1 mashed avocado to make the tuna salad extra creamy, or add diced tomatoes, red onion, and celery for more crunch and flavor. If you don't have rainbow chard leaves, you could try collard greens, kale, or romaine lettuce.

PER SERVING: Calories: 309; Total fat: 18g; Saturated fat: 3g; Sodium: 1325mg; Carbohydrates: 25g; Fiber: 6g; Sugar: 15g; Protein: 16g

GREEN VEGGIE SANDWICH

QUICK

SERVES 2
PREP TIME: 10 minutes

1 avocado
4 slices whole-grain
   bread, toasted
½ cucumber, thinly sliced
1 cup alfalfa sprouts
1 cup baby spinach
1 teaspoon freshly
   squeezed lemon juice
Sea salt
Freshly ground
   black pepper

Sprouts and microgreens are the baby versions of plants just after bursting from the seed. This is when they contain the highest levels of micronutrients, oftentimes even more than the mature version of the plant. Adding sprouts and microgreens to your sandwiches, soups, salads, and stir-fries can take your meals to the next level.

1. Mash ¼ of the avocado onto each slice of toast.

2. Layer the cucumber slices on 2 of the slices of bread and push down gently so the cucumber slices sink into the avocado.

3. Add the sprouts and spinach on top of the cucumber slices.

4. Season with the lemon juice and salt and pepper to taste.

5. Top with the other two slices of toast.

VARIATION TIP: To add protein to this meal, you could mash cooked white navy or cannellini beans with the avocado, or layer on Hummus (page 122), baked tofu (see page 72), or Soft "Cheese" Spread (page 127).

PER SERVING: Calories: 346; Total fat: 14g; Saturated fat: 2g; Sodium: 411mg; Carbohydrates: 46g; Fiber: 11g; Sugar: 5g; Protein: 14g

BAKED TOFU PESTO PANINI

SERVES 4

PREP TIME: 10 minutes, plus 5 minutes to press the tofu

COOK TIME: 30 minutes

14 ounces extra-firm tofu
4 tablespoons
   extra-virgin olive
   oil, divided
½ teaspoon garlic powder
½ teaspoon
   onion powder
½ teaspoon
   dried oregano
4 Roma tomatoes, halved
½ teaspoon sea salt
½ teaspoon freshly
   ground black pepper
4 whole wheat
   ciabatta buns
1 cup Perfect Pesto
   (page 128)
2 cups baby spinach
½ cup fresh basil leaves
   (optional)

Pressed paninis originated in the sandwich shops of Italy in the 1960s and became popular as a quick lunch for office workers. In general, a panini contains only three or four ingredients, so they work well for keeping things simple on a plant-based diet.

1. Preheat the oven to 375°F.

2. Remove the tofu from the package and wrap it in a clean cloth or paper towels. Place the tofu on a plate and add a second plate on top. Weigh down the top plate with a few heavy cans and leave the tofu to "press" for 5 minutes.

3. In a medium bowl, mix 1 tablespoon of olive oil, the garlic powder, the onion powder, and the oregano.

4. Unwrap the tofu from the towel and slice into ¼-inch-thick patties. Coat each patty in the oil-and-spice mixture.

5. Place the patties on a rimmed baking sheet and bake them in the oven for 25 minutes, flipping them over after 15 minutes (they're ready to flip when they no longer stick to the pan).

6. In a single layer on another rimmed baking sheet, place the tomatoes cut-side up, drizzle with 2 tablespoons of olive oil, season with the salt and pepper, then toss the tomatoes to evenly coat them. Bake in the oven for 20 minutes.

7. Cut the ciabatta buns in half and spread each side with ¼ cup pesto.

8. Remove the trays from the oven. Lay one tofu patty on each ciabatta bun bottom and top with 1 roasted tomato, ¼ cup spinach, and ⅛ cup basil, if using.

9. Place the top bun over the filling and brush the exterior of each bun with the remaining 1 tablespoon of olive oil.

10. In a panini press, if you have one, grill each sandwich for 5 minutes. Otherwise, grill each sandwich in a pan on medium-high heat for 3 to 4 minutes on each side.

PREP TIP: Try panfrying the tofu instead of baking it to save an extra 10 minutes of cooking time.

VARIATION TIP: Spread some Soft "Cheese" Spread (page 127) on each bun before grilling the sandwich.

PER SERVING: Calories: 624; Total fat: 43g; Saturated fat: 6g; Sodium: 557mg; Carbohydrates: 39g; Fiber: 8g; Sugar: 4g; Protein: 23g

Mediterranean
Buddha Bowl,
page **76**

CHAPTER 6

VEGETARIAN MAINS AND SIDES

MEDITERRANEAN BUDDHA BOWL

QUICK

SERVES 2
PREP TIME: 20 minutes

3 cups mixed greens
1 cup cooked quinoa
1 cup chickpeas, drained
  and rinsed
⅔ cup Hummus (page 122)
½ cucumber, seeded
  and diced
1 cup cherry
  tomatoes, halved
½ cup kalamata
  olives, halved
½ cup diced orange
  bell pepper

"Buddha bowls" are among the most versatile ways to enjoy a healthy meal. They usually consist of a base of leafy greens, plus whole grains, some protein, and loads of different vegetables with a dip or sauce of your choosing. All sorts of international themes and flavors work well for a Buddha bowl, and you can also improvise with the ingredients you have on hand. In this recipe, we're going to stick with a combination of Mediterranean ingredients and flavors.

1. Divide the greens evenly between 2 bowls and top each with ½ the quinoa, chickpeas, hummus, cucumber, cherry tomatoes, olives, and bell pepper.

2. Toss to combine.

INGREDIENT TIP: It can be easy to overdo it when making this meal, as the calories can quickly add up, especially with sauce options. Just be sure that your bowl contains double the amount of vegetables as protein and grains, and you'll be able to keep it within a healthy portion size.

VARIATION TIP: Tzatziki (page 130), Perfect Pesto (page 128), tofu "chorizo" (see page 46), avocado, or any vegetables of your choosing all make excellent extra toppings. Use whole-grain couscous if you're in a pinch and don't have any precooked quinoa, as couscous cooks in just a few minutes.

PER SERVING: Calories: 550; Total fat: 28g; Saturated fat: 4g; Sodium: 1318mg; Carbohydrates: 63g; Fiber: 17g; Sugar: 11g; Protein: 18g

WHITE BEAN ZUCCHINI ALFREDO

GLUTEN-FREE, QUICK

SERVES 2
PREP TIME: 10 minutes
COOK TIME: 10 minutes

2 zucchini, ends trimmed
1 (16-ounce) can cooked
  white cannellini beans,
  drained and rinsed
1 garlic clove
2 tablespoons chopped
  fresh parsley
¼ cup nutritional yeast
¾ to 1 cup unsweetened
  nondairy milk, divided
¼ cup Parmesan
  "Cheese" (page 126)

Traditional Alfredo sauce is made with heavy cream, butter, and Parmesan cheese. From a health standpoint, it's pretty heavy on unhealthy fats. Fortunately, you can enjoy this dairy-free, protein-rich version made with white cannellini beans.

1. Using a spiralizer, create noodles out of the zucchini. Set aside.

2. In a blender or food processor combine the beans, garlic, parsley, nutritional yeast, and ¾ cup of milk.

3. Blend until smooth, adding ¼ cup of milk if you want a thinner Alfredo sauce.

4. Transfer the bean sauce to a medium saucepan over low heat.

5. While the sauce warms, in a large skillet over medium heat, gently sauté the zucchini noodles, about 5 minutes, until they are a little softer and less crunchy.

6. Divide the zucchini noodles between 2 plates, top with the Alfredo sauce, and sprinkle with 2 tablespoons of Parmesan "Cheese."

VARIATION TIP: You can mix in your favorite sautéed vegetables like onions, mushrooms, cherry tomatoes, and peppers with the zucchini noodles, and sprinkle red chili flakes on top to spice it up. Navy beans, great northern beans, or baby lima beans can replace the cannellini beans.

PER SERVING: Calories: 383; Total fat: 10g; Saturated fat: 1g; Sodium: 161mg; Carbohydrates: 49g; Fiber: 17g; Sugar: 8g; Protein: 29g

PASTA WITH LENTIL-BEET BALLS

SERVES 2

PREP TIME: 20 minutes

COOK TIME: 20 minutes, plus 5 minutes for cooling

1 tablespoon flaxseed

3 tablespoons water

2 garlic cloves

1 tablespoon dried basil

1 tablespoon
  dried oregano

1 tablespoon
  dried parsley

1 cup cooked red lentils,
  drained and cooled

1 cup steamed beets,
  drained well and cooled

¼ cup quick oats

6 ounces dried
  whole-grain spaghetti

1 tablespoon
  tomato paste

1¼ cups tomato sauce

Parmesan "Cheese"
  (page 126)

Spaghetti and meatballs are typically made with refined flour pasta and ground beef. In this plant-based variation, the lentils not only sub in for the meat but also provide plant-based iron, a mineral crucial to energy levels, nutrient transportation, and even healthy blood cells. Beets, meanwhile, are rich in health-protecting antioxidants and vitamin C to help with iron absorption.

1. Preheat the oven to 375°F.

2. In a food processor, blend together the flaxseed, water, garlic, basil, oregano, and parsley. Let sit for 2 to 3 minutes to allow the flaxseed to become gelatinous, like egg whites.

3. Add the lentils and beets to the food processor and pulse until combined, but not pureed. If the mixture is too thin, stir in 1 tablespoon of oats at a time until the mixture is thick and doughy.

4. Scoop out 1 tablespoon of the mixture and roll into a ball. It should stick together enough to make a ball but feel fragile. Continue making the balls until the all the beet mixture is used. You should have 12 lentil-beet balls.

5. Heat the lentil-beet balls on a rimmed baking sheet in the oven for 20 minutes.

6. Prepare the pasta according to the package directions while the lentil-beet balls are baking.

7. In a medium saucepan, warm the tomato paste and sauce over medium heat, stirring so it doesn't burn.

8. Remove the lentil-beet balls from the oven and allow to cool for 5 minutes before lifting them from the tray.

9. Divide the pasta between 2 plates. Add 6 lentil-beet balls to each plate, top with the tomato sauce, and sprinkle the Parmesan "Cheese" over each plate.

PREP TIP: Cook a double or triple batch of the lentil-beet balls and store them in the freezer for up to 3 months, so that they are always available for a quick meal.

VARIATION TIP: Use canned red lentils and canned beets instead of cooking them yourself and use 3 tablespoons of Italian seasoning (page 50) instead of individually measuring out 3 different spices.

PER SERVING: Calories: 559; Total fat: 4g; Saturated fat: 1g; Sodium: 803mg; Carbohydrates: 112g; Fiber: 20g; Sugar: 13g; Protein: 28g

VEGAN PAELLA

SERVES 4
PREP TIME: 15 minutes
COOK TIME: 25 minutes

4 cups Vegetable Broth
  (page 123)
1 teaspoon paella spice
1 tablespoon extra-virgin
  olive oil
⅔ cup diced yellow onion
4 garlic cloves, minced
1 cup diced red
  bell pepper
3 cups medium-grain rice
2 tablespoons freshly
  squeezed lemon juice
1 cup frozen peas
1 (16-ounce) can white
  cannellini beans
1 batch tofu "chorizo"
  (see page 46), optional

PER SERVING: Calories:
713; Total fat: 5g; Saturated
fat: 1g; Sodium: 646mg;
Carbohydrates: 145g; Fiber:
9g; Sugar: 8g; Protein: 18g

Originating from Valencia, Spain, paella typically includes seafood and can take more than an hour to prepare in a special pan on an open-flame grill. But you can keep this recipe as easy as possible with what you have at home. The two most important ingredients for great paella are rice and spices. The rice should be medium grain so that it's highly absorbent and takes on the spice blend nicely.

1. In a medium saucepan over low heat, combine the vegetable broth and paella spice and bring to a simmer. Do not let the mixture boil.

2. In a large deep skillet, heat the olive oil over medium heat. Sauté the onion, garlic, and bell pepper for 2 to 3 minutes, until the onion is translucent.

3. Add the rice to the pan and sauté for 2 minutes, stirring. Add the warm vegetable broth and the lemon juice. Stir to combine and reduce the heat to medium-low.

4. Bring to a simmer and cook for 10 minutes, or until almost all the broth is absorbed by the rice and it is slightly tender.

5. Add in the frozen peas, cannellini beans, and tofu "chorizo" (if using), and mix well to combine.

Continued >

6. Reduce the heat to low, cover the pan, and continue to cook for an additional 5 to 10 minutes, or until the rice is tender.

INGREDIENT TIP: You can find paella spice in the international aisle of your grocery store or make your own with the following spices: 1 pinch ground saffron, 1 tablespoon paprika, 1 teaspoon onion powder, 1 teaspoon garlic powder, ½ teaspoon cayenne pepper, and ½ teaspoon freshly ground black pepper.

PREP TIP: You can cut the cooking time by using quinoa or couscous in place of the rice, be sure to use a highly absorbent grain. The key to this recipe is in the spice, so stick with the paella spice mix and you'll be on your way to enjoying a delicious Spanish-inspired dish.

VARIATION TIP: Use any vegetables you have on hand and consider adding in a few cups of chopped leafy greens at step 5.

PUMPKIN MAC 'N' CHEESE

SERVES 4
PREP TIME: 5 minutes
COOK TIME: 15 minutes

2 cups dried macaroni
    noodles
1½ cups unsweetened
    nondairy milk
2 teaspoons
    garlic powder
½ cup nutritional yeast
2 teaspoons
    Dijon mustard
1 cup canned
    pumpkin puree
1 (16-ounce) can white
    navy beans, drained
    and rinsed
Sea salt
Freshly ground
    black pepper

This creative dish shows off how vegetables can transform a recipe, while giving an American favorite a plant-based, Mediterranean-inspired twist. The "cheese" sauce uses pumpkin for a smooth, creamy base, meaning it has fewer calories and plenty of fiber. Feel free to sprinkle some red chili flakes or Parmesan "Cheese" (page 126) on top.

1. Cook the noodles according to the package directions.

2. While the pasta cooks, in a medium saucepan over medium heat, warm the milk.

3. Add the garlic powder, nutritional yeast, mustard, and pumpkin puree to the milk and whisk until well combined.

4. Turn the heat down to low and cook for 5 minutes.

5. In a blender, combine 1 cup of the pumpkin mixture with the navy beans.

6. Blend until smooth and then pour back into the saucepan and mix well.

7. Pour the sauce over the cooked, drained macaroni noodles, stir, and season with salt and pepper to taste.

VARIATION TIP: Try using silken or soft tofu if you don't have any white beans.

PER SERVING: Calories: 444; Total fat: 3g; Saturated fat: <1g; Sodium: 137mg; Carbohydrates: 80g; Fiber: 16g; Sugar: 5g; Protein: 24g

ONE-PAN ROSEMARY-ROASTED TOFU

GLUTEN-FREE

SERVES 4
PREP TIME: 5 minutes
COOK TIME: 25 minutes

14 ounces extra-firm tofu
1 tablespoon extra-virgin
   olive oil
1 tablespoon low-sodium
   soy sauce
½ teaspoon garlic powder
1 teaspoon finely chopped
   dried rosemary
2 tablespoons
   cornstarch, divided

Roasting tofu with garlic and rosemary (popular flavors for chicken) is one of my favorite ways to make it. An excellent protein, tofu helps keep you feeling satisfied and energized while reducing your appetite.

1. Remove the tofu from the package and wrap in a clean cloth or paper towels. Place the tofu on a plate and add a second plate on top. Weigh down the top plate with a few heavy cans and leave the tofu to "press" for 5 minutes.

2. Preheat the oven to 400°F.

3. In a medium mixing bowl, whisk together the olive oil, soy sauce, garlic powder, rosemary, and 1 tablespoon of cornstarch until smooth.

4. Cut the tofu block in half lengthwise and then cut each rectangle into about 16 pieces.

5. Toss the tofu in the sauce and stir well to combine. Add the remaining 1 tablespoon of cornstarch to the mix and stir well.

6. Lay the tofu cubes on a baking sheet in a single layer and cook in the oven for 25 minutes, flipping them at the 15-minute mark.

INGREDIENT TIP: Pressing the liquid out of the tofu helps to cook the tofu quicker and prevents an overly chewy texture.

PAIRING TIP: Serve with Quinoa-Stuffed Peppers (page 86), the Mediterranean Buddha Bowl (page 76), or Garlic-Roasted Veggies (page 88).

PER SERVING: Calories: 155; Total fat: 9g; Saturated fat: 1g; Sodium: 226mg; Carbohydrates: 8g; Fiber: 1g; Sugar: 0g; Protein: 11g

ROASTED GARLIC AND CAULIFLOWER MASH

GLUTEN-FREE

SERVES 4
PREP TIME: 10 minutes
COOK TIME: 20 minutes

4 cups cauliflower, raw or
   frozen defrosted
4 garlic cloves, peeled
2 tablespoons, plus
   1 teaspoon extra-virgin
   olive oil, divided
1 teaspoon dried thyme
¼ teaspoon sea salt
¼ cup unsweetened
   nondairy milk

Cauliflower is part of the brassica family of plants, which includes broccoli, kale, Brussels sprouts, and cabbage—all are good sources of calcium in a plant-based diet. While cauliflower does contain less calcium than its greener cousins, it makes for a really tasty alternative to heavier mashed potatoes.

1. Preheat the oven to 375°F.

2. Chop the cauliflower into smaller florets.

3. In a large bowl, toss the florets and whole garlic with 2 tablespoons of olive oil, the thyme, and the salt.

4. On a large, rimmed baking sheet, arrange the garlic and cauliflower and roast them in the oven for 20 minutes, stirring after 10 minutes.

5. Remove the roasted vegetables from the oven and put them into a blender with the milk and 1 teaspoon of olive oil.

6. Blend until smooth, or to your desired mashed consistency.

PAIRING TIP: This dish makes an excellent side for Chicken Souvlaki (page 103) or One-Pan Rosemary-Roasted Tofu (page 84).

LEFTOVERS TIP: Try it as a topping for a veggie shepherd's pie in place of mashed potatoes.

PER SERVING: Calories: 104; Total fat: 8g; Saturated fat: 1g; Sodium: 190mg; Carbohydrates: 7g; Fiber: 2g; Sugar: 2g; Protein: 2g

QUINOA-STUFFED PEPPERS

GLUTEN-FREE

SERVES 6
PREP TIME: 15 minutes
COOK TIME: 30 minutes

1 cup uncooked quinoa,
  rinsed and drained
2 cups water
6 bell peppers (red, green,
  orange, and yellow),
  deveined, seeded, and
  halved lengthwise
2 tablespoons extra-virgin
  olive oil
4 garlic cloves, minced
1 small onion, diced
1 teaspoon red chili flakes
1 teaspoon dried oregano
2 tablespoons freshly
  squeezed lemon juice
¼ cup chopped fresh
  parsley

Usually stuffed peppers contain meat and cheese and run high in calories, saturated fats, and oils. But this healthier, low-carb version is an appealing alternative, with the quinoa providing complex carbohydrates to give you energy and proteins that help you feel full. Use a variety of colored peppers to make this meal look just as beautiful as it tastes.

1. Preheat the oven to 425°F.

2. In a medium saucepan with a lid, bring the quinoa and water to a boil over high heat. Lower the heat and cover the saucepan. Simmer the quinoa for about 15 minutes while you prepare the rest of the recipe.

3. In a rimmed baking sheet, place the bell peppers cut-side down, and bake for 15 minutes.

4. In a large skillet over medium heat, heat the olive oil. Add the garlic, onion, and red chili flakes and sauté for 3 to 4 minutes, or until the garlic is fragrant.

5. Add the oregano, lemon juice, and parsley and sauté for 1 more minute.

6. Add the cooked quinoa to the skillet and combine.

7. Remove the peppers from the oven and flip them over.

8. Scoop the quinoa mixture into the open peppers and return them to the oven for an additional 5 minutes.

9. Allow the peppers to cool for 5 minutes before serving.

PREP TIP: You can prepare the quinoa mixture ahead of time, then cook the stuffed peppers in the slow cooker for 4 hours on low to have this meal waiting for you when you get home from a busy day. You may want to add 1 cup of water to the bottom of your slow cooker to ensure there is enough moisture in the pot to cook the peppers.

VARIATION TIP: You can pour tomato sauce onto each pepper after filling them with the quinoa mixture for a "saucy" take on this meal, and top it with Parmesan "Cheese" (page 126) just before serving. Or swap out some, or all, of the quinoa in this recipe for cooked brown lentils or crumbled extra-firm tofu.

PER SERVING: Calories: 194; Total fat: 7g; Saturated fat: 1g; Sodium: 11mg; Carbohydrates: 30g; Fiber: 6g; Sugar: 8g; Protein: 5g

GARLIC-ROASTED VEGGIES

GLUTEN-FREE

SERVES 4
PREP TIME: 15 minutes
COOK TIME: 30 minutes

1 large sweet potato
2 medium beets
2 medium carrots
1 zucchini
2 tablespoons extra-virgin
  olive oil
2 tablespoons
  balsamic vinegar
4 garlic cloves, minced
2 teaspoons dried basil
2 teaspoons
  dried oregano
2 cups cremini
  mushrooms
1 red onion, chopped
Sea salt
Freshly ground
  black pepper

Sheet-pan veggies are a fun way to add color and variety to your plate without a lot of hands-on work. I recommend cleaning your vegetables really well so that you don't have to peel them, because the peel contains higher levels of micronutrients than the flesh inside.

1. Preheat the oven to 425°F.

2. Dice the sweet potato, beets, carrots, and zucchini into ½-inch cubes.

3. In a small bowl, whisk together the olive oil, balsamic vinegar, garlic, basil, and oregano.

4. On a rimmed baking sheet, spread the diced vegetables, the mushrooms, and the onion in a single layer and drizzle the oil mixture over the vegetables. Toss to evenly coat, and season with salt and pepper to taste.

5. Roast in the oven for 15 minutes.

6. Stir the vegetables after 15 minutes and continue roasting them for an additional 10 to 15 minutes, or until the vegetables are tender.

VARIATION TIP: Consider adding rutabaga, turnips, parsnips, cauliflower, broccoli, or Brussels sprouts. You can also change up the flavors by using different spices like dill or tarragon, or even cinnamon for a sweeter twist.

PER SERVING: Calories: 177; Total fat: 7g; Saturated fat: 1g; Sodium: 92mg; Carbohydrates: 25g; Fiber: 5g; Sugar: 11g; Protein: 5g

MEDITERRANEAN FETTUCCINE

SERVES 2
PREP TIME: 5 minutes
COOK TIME: 20 minutes

4 ounces dried fettuccine
2 cups finely chopped
  kale leaves
¼ cup kalamata olives
1 tablespoon freshly
  squeezed lemon juice
2 tablespoons extra-virgin
  olive oil
1 tablespoon
  nutritional yeast
⅛ teaspoon sea salt

This simple meal comes together with ease and can be customized by adding additional spices, such as garlic or chile peppers. Kale is known to be high in vitamins C and K, and is another delicious source of plant-based calcium. To experience the benefits of the calcium, lightly cooking kale—as is done in this recipe—will deactivate the known anti-nutrients that inhibit calcium absorption.

1. Cook the pasta according to the package directions. Once the pasta is cooked and drained, rinse under cold water to prevent overcooking. Set aside.

2. In the same pot used for the pasta, cook the kale and olives over medium heat for 3 to 4 minutes, until the kale is soft and bright green.

3. Add the pasta back to the pot along with the lemon juice, olive oil, nutritional yeast, and salt. Toss to combine.

INGREDIENT TIP: Remove the hard and fibrous stems from the kale leaves, and then give the leaves a quick massage for 1 minute to break up the fibers and make the kale easier to chew and digest.

VARIATION TIP: Eliminate the gluten by using gluten-free (such as brown rice) fettuccine noodles. Add a batch of One-Pan Rosemary-Roasted Tofu (page 84) or lentil-beet balls (see page 78) for more protein. Parmesan "Cheese" (page 126) can also be used in place of nutritional yeast.

PER SERVING: Calories: 382; Total fat: 18g; Saturated fat: 2g; Sodium: 397mg; Carbohydrates: 46g; Fiber: 5g; Sugar: 2g; Protein: 10g

BROCCOLI AND CHICKPEA COUSCOUS

QUICK

SERVES 2
PREP TIME: 5 minutes
COOK TIME: 15 minutes

3 garlic cloves, minced
4½ tablespoons
   extra-virgin olive
   oil, divided
1½ cups Vegetable Broth
   (page 123), divided
1 cup whole-grain
   couscous
3 cups broccoli, chopped
   into florets
1 (16-ounce) can
   chickpeas, drained
   and rinsed
3 tablespoons freshly
   squeezed lemon juice
4 tablespoons
   fresh parsley
Sea salt
Freshly ground
   black pepper

This combination works as a main or a side—and the perfect potluck dish—plus you can throw it together in no time. The chickpeas offer protein to help you feel full, while the broccoli provides plenty of phytonutrients to support overall good health. You'll love how delicious these simple flavors can be, especially after marinating in the refrigerator for a day, so feel free to make enough for leftovers. It can be served warm or cold.

1. In a medium saucepan, sauté the garlic in ½ tablespoon of olive oil on medium-low heat until fragrant, about 3 minutes.

2. Add the vegetable broth and couscous to the saucepan and cook on low for 3 to 5 minutes until the broth is absorbed, and the couscous is soft and fluffy.

3. In a medium skillet, heat 1 tablespoon of olive oil over high heat and sauté the broccoli for 5 minutes.

4. Add the chickpeas to the broccoli, stir together, and cook for another 5 minutes, until the chickpeas are warmed through.

5. Combine the cooked couscous with the broccoli-and-chickpea mixture.

6. Add the remaining 3 tablespoons of olive oil, lemon juice, and parsley, and stir. Season with salt and pepper to taste.

PER SERVING: Calories: 826; Total fat: 36g; Saturated fat: 5g; Sodium: 835mg; Carbohydrates: 105g; Fiber: 17g; Sugar: 14g; Protein: 26g

THREE-BEAN CHILI

GLUTEN-FREE

SERVES 4
PREP TIME: 10 minutes
COOK TIME: 30 minutes

2 tablespoons extra-virgin
  olive oil
1 yellow onion, diced
4 garlic cloves, minced
¼ cup tomato paste
2 teaspoons chili powder
1 teaspoon cumin
1 teaspoon paprika
1 cup Vegetable Broth
  (page 123)
1 (16 ounce) can diced
  tomatoes, drained
2 (16 ounce) cans mixed
  beans, or about 4 cups
  of cooked chickpeas,
  red kidney beans, and
  white cannellini beans

Chili is not only comforting, filling, and delicious but also an inexpensive way to feed a large crowd, and it's a natural for repurposing leftovers. See the tips below for ideas on more add-ins that you may have hiding in your refrigerator.

1. In a large stockpot over medium heat, heat the olive oil. Add the onion and garlic and sauté for about 4 minutes, or until fragrant.

2. Add the tomato paste, chili powder, cumin, and paprika and cook for 1 minute more.

3. Deglaze the pot with the vegetable broth, scraping the bottom, and stir well.

4. Add the diced tomatoes and mixed beans, stir well, and simmer on medium-low heat for 25 minutes, stirring occasionally to keep the bottom from burning.

PREP TIP: To make this in a slow cooker, after completing step 3, pour everything into the slow cooker, give it a really good stir to combine, and then cover and cook on low for 3 to 4 hours.

VARIATION TIP: Use any mixture of beans that you have available, or even a combination of lentils and whole grains like spelt and farro. You can also sauté any other chopped vegetables that you like, such as bell peppers, broccoli, sweet potato cubes, and corn.

PER SERVING: Calories: 328; Total fat: 11g; Saturated fat: 1g; Sodium: 791mg; Carbohydrates: 46g; Fiber: 13g; Sugar: 11g; Protein: 13g

Pesto
Shrimp Pasta,
page **98**

CHAPTER 7

SEAFOOD AND POULTRY MAINS

SAUERKRAUT-CRUSTED SALMON

SERVES 2
PREP TIME: 10 minutes
COOK TIME: 15 minutes

¼ cup sauerkraut
2 tablespoons
   whole-grain
   Dijon mustard
2 teaspoons extra-virgin
   olive oil, divided
2 (6-ounce) salmon fillets
Sea salt
Freshly ground
   black pepper

Our gut is sometimes called our "second brain." So it stands to reason that we should take good care of our digestive system. This gut-healthy dish features probiotic-rich grilled sauerkraut—an ingredient that's been shown in some studies to improve digestion, immunity, and mood—on a flaky fillet of salmon that's loaded with omega-3 fatty acids.

1. Preheat the oven to 375°F.

2. In a small bowl, mix the sauerkraut and mustard.

3. In a medium skillet, warm 1 teaspoon of olive oil over high heat.

4. Spread the sauerkraut mixture on one side of each salmon fillet and cook the fillets, sauerkraut-side down, in the skillet for 8 minutes.

5. Flip the fillets and transfer them to a baking dish. Bake in the oven for an additional 8 minutes.

6. Remove the salmon from the oven and allow to cool for 5 minutes before plating and serving with your side of choice. Add salt and pepper, to taste.

PAIRING TIP: This dish goes well with brown rice and the Roasted Garlic and Cauliflower Mash (page 85) or Garlic-Roasted Veggies (page 88).

LEFTOVERS TIP: The cooked salmon fillets can be refrigerated for up to 3 days and added to salads or Buddha bowls.

PER SERVING: Calories: 240; Total fat: 11g; Saturated fat: 3g; Sodium: 690mg; Carbohydrates: 1g; Fiber: 1g; Sugar: 3g; Protein: 33g

ONE-POT WHITEFISH AND RICE

SERVES 4
PREP TIME: 5 minutes
COOK TIME: 15 minutes

1½ cups whole-grain
  basmati rice, rinsed
2¼ cups water
2 cups cherry
  tomatoes, chopped
1 tablespoon apple
  cider vinegar
1 cup chopped basil
  leaves, divided
½ cup kalamata olives
½ teaspoon sea salt
½ teaspoon freshly
  ground black pepper
2 haddock fillets, cut
  into thirds
2 cups baby
  spinach leaves

The countries along the coast of the Mediterranean Sea include plenty of fish in their diet as a protein source. Haddock packs a lot of minerals, including selenium, magnesium, and zinc, that can help build bone strength, regulate your heart rate, and promote overall health.

1. In a large pot with a lid, over high heat, combine the rice and water. Cover and bring to a boil, then lower the heat and simmer the rice.

2. In a medium bowl, mix the tomatoes, vinegar, ½ cup of basil leaves, the olives, salt, and pepper.

3. Arrange the fish pieces over the rice after it's been simmering for a few minutes. Pour the tomato-basil mixture over the fillet pieces and cover. Simmer for 10 minutes.

4. Add the spinach leaves in an even layer to the pot over the fillets and simmer for another 5 minutes, or until the rice and fish are cooked through, adding more water if necessary.

5. Garnish with the remaining ½ cup basil leaves and serve.

VARIATION TIP: Use another type or brown or wild rice if you don't have whole-grain basmati rice on hand to improve the carbohydrate content of this meal.

PER SERVING: Calories: 347; Total fat: 6; Saturated fat: 1g; Sodium: 827mg; Carbohydrates: 54g; Fiber: 5g; Sugar: 3g; Protein: 24g

ONE-POT MEDITERRANEAN MACKEREL PASTA

QUICK

SERVES 4
PREP TIME: 5 minutes
COOK TIME: 15 minutes

2 tablespoons extra-virgin olive oil
2 garlic cloves, minced
4 ounces canned mackerel, skinless and boneless
½ teaspoon chili flakes
8 ounces dried whole-grain linguine noodles
3 cups water
½ cup pitted green olives
Sea salt
Freshly ground black pepper
2 tablespoons freshly squeezed lemon juice
¼ cup fresh parsley, finely chopped

Mackerel contains a healthy portion of omega-3 fatty acids and vitamin D, which promotes longevity and decreased inflammation within the body, and even helps maintain beautiful skin. This dish brings together traditional Mediterranean ingredients while reducing your time in the kitchen by keeping them all in one pot.

1. In a large saucepan with a lid, warm the olive oil over medium-high heat. Add the garlic to the hot oil and cook until fragrant, 1 to 2 minutes, stirring often to prevent the garlic from burning. Break the mackerel into pieces, then add the mackerel and chili flakes and stir until warmed through.

2. Add the pasta and water to the saucepan. Cover and bring to a boil and cook the pasta for 8 to 10 minutes, stirring to keep the pasta from sticking.

3. Add a splash of water if the pasta seems too dry, or use a ladle to remove excess water once the pasta is cooked through.

4. Stir in the olives and season with salt and pepper to taste. Mix well. Divide between 4 plates, sprinkle with the lemon juice, and garnish with the fresh parsley.

VARIATION TIP: Use freshly cooked mackerel fillets in place of canned or swap the mackerel for the One-Pan Rosemary-Roasted Tofu (page 84).

PER SERVING: Calories: 338; Total fat: 13g; Saturated fat: 2g; Sodium: 425mg; Carbohydrates: 44g; Fiber: 6g; Sugar: 2g; Protein: 15g

ONE-PAN MEDITERRANEAN TROUT

SERVES 4
PREP TIME: 10 minutes
COOK TIME: 15 minutes

2 cups basil leaves
Juice of ½ lemon
2 garlic cloves
¼ cup hemp hearts
¼ teaspoon sea salt
¼ cup extra-virgin
   olive oil
4 trout fillets (about
   5 ounces each)
2 cups canned artichoke
   hearts, drained, rinsed,
   and chopped
½ cup assorted olives
4 tomatoes, chopped

Here Mediterranean vegetables come together with trout fillets for a lively plate. Artichokes—which are actually immature flower buds, harvested before they blossom—are time-consuming to prepare when fresh, so this recipe uses canned artichokes, packed in water with low sodium.

1. Preheat the oven to 450°F. Line a rimmed baking sheet with parchment paper.

2. Combine the basil, lemon juice, garlic, hemp hearts, salt, and olive oil in a food processor. Pulse until smooth.

3. Place the trout fillets on the prepared baking sheet and arrange the artichoke hearts, olives, and tomatoes on the pan.

4. Top each fillet with a generous amount of the basil mixture.

5. Bake for about 15 minutes, or until the trout is thoroughly cooked.

PREP TIP: Whole cherry tomatoes will work instead of chopped ones, and will save you some prep time.

PAIRING TIP: You can side this meal with rice, quinoa, or couscous to add some grains and extra calories.

PER SERVING: Calories: 484; Total fat: 32g; Saturated fat: 4g; Sodium: 830mg; Carbohydrates: 18g; Fiber: 11g; Sugar: 4g; Protein: 38g

PESTO SHRIMP PASTA

QUICK

SERVES 4
PREP TIME: 5 minutes
COOK TIME: 15 minutes

8 ounces dried
   whole-grain fettuccine
1 pound shrimp, peeled
   and deveined
¼ teaspoon sea salt
⅓ cup Perfect Pesto
   (page 128)
Juice of 1 lemon
¼ teaspoon red
   chili flakes
2 tablespoons finely
   chopped fresh parsley

A seafood favorite is the star of this simple, zesty pasta dish. Low in carbohydrates and calories, but still packed with nutrients, shrimp can be an ideal choice if you're trying to shed some pounds.

1. In a large saucepan, cook the pasta according to the package directions. Save ½ cup of the pasta water before draining the finished pasta.

2. Cook the pasta until al dente. Set aside.

3. In a medium skillet over medium heat, warm the ½ cup reserved pasta water. Add the shrimp to the pan and cook for about 2 minutes per side, or until the shrimp is no longer translucent.

4. Season with the salt.

5. In a large bowl, combine the pasta, cooked shrimp, pesto, lemon juice, chili flakes, and parsley and stir well to combine.

PREP TIP: Buying precooked, frozen shrimp can save you a step. Defrost the shrimp while the pasta is cooking and mix it all in the pot when the pasta is ready.

PER SERVING: Calories: 369; Total fat: 12g; Saturated fat: 2g; Sodium: 1003mg; Carbohydrates: 47g; Fiber: 6g; Sugar: 2g; Protein: 25g

CHICKEN MOUSSAKA

SERVES 4
PREP TIME: 10 minutes
COOK TIME: 35 minutes

FOR THE MOUSSAKA

1 eggplant, cubed
¼ cup extra-virgin olive
   oil, divided
1 pound lean
   ground chicken
⅔ yellow onion, diced
3 garlic cloves, minced
⅛ teaspoon sea salt
1 (16-ounce) can diced
   tomatoes
1 tablespoon
   tomato paste
1 teaspoon paprika
¾ cup water, as needed

FOR THE BÉCHAMEL
SAUCE (OPTIONAL)

⅓ cup extra-virgin
   olive oil
⅓ cup all-purpose flour
2 cups unsweetened
   nondairy milk
Sea salt
Freshly ground
   black pepper

Moussaka, originating in Turkey and adopted by Greece, typically features a vegetable bake, usually potato or eggplant, with a tomato and ground lamb meat sauce. This recipe subs in chicken for lamb and takes a few shortcuts, as traditional moussaka can take upward of 2 hours to prepare. The optional, updated French béchamel sauce helps to balance and lend richness to the dish.

1. Preheat the oven to 400°F.

2. Place the eggplant on a rimmed baking sheet, toss with ⅛ cup of olive oil, and roast in the oven for about 20 minutes, or until tender.

3. In a large saucepan over high heat, brown the ground chicken until cooked through, then remove from the pan and set aside.

4. In the same pan, heat the remaining ⅛ cup of olive oil and sauté the onion and garlic for 5 to 6 minutes, until the onion is translucent and soft.

5. Add the cooked chicken, salt, diced tomatoes, tomato paste, paprika and roasted eggplant. Stir, lower the heat, and bring to a simmer. Cook for about 15 minutes, adding water as needed, until you reach your desired consistency.

Continued >

6. To make the béchamel sauce (if using): In a small saucepan over medium heat, heat the olive oil. Add the flour and milk, and whisk the mixture well so no clumps form. Continue whisking to prevent the sauce from burning. The sauce is finished when it has thickened. Season with salt and pepper to taste.

7. Divide the chicken moussaka between 4 plates, top with the béchamel sauce, and allow to cool for 5 minutes before eating.

PREP TIP: To make this in a slow cooker, after completing steps 1 through 3, add the cooked eggplant and the chicken, onion, and garlic to your slow cooker. Allow the ingredients to cook and marinate for 4 hours on low before continuing with step 5.

VARIATION TIP: To make this vegan, use cooked lentils or crumbled extra-firm tofu instead of ground chicken. If you're not eating gluten, use gluten-free flour or omit the sauce entirely. To make this meal a little heartier, especially on cold days, replace half the eggplant with white or yellow potatoes.

PER SERVING: Calories: 364; Total fat: 23g; Saturated fat: 4g; Sodium: 346mg; Carbohydrates: 16g; Fiber: 7g; Sugar: 9g; Protein: 25g

ONE-PAN CHICKEN, BROCCOLI, AND PEPPERS

GLUTEN-FREE

SERVES 4
PREP TIME: 10 minutes
COOK TIME: 20 minutes

¼ cup extra-virgin olive oil, divided
¼ cup white wine vinegar
2 teaspoons Dijon mustard
1 teaspoon sea salt, divided
8 cups broccoli, chopped into small florets
4 orange bell peppers, thinly sliced
4 boneless, skinless chicken breasts, sliced into strips

A Dijon-spiked roasting sauce adds flavor to this simple meal, which can easily be modified by adding different spices or swapping the vegetables for what you have available. This recipe works great as a main dish with a side of brown rice, as an added layer to a salad, or as a delicious filling for a wrap or pita, or a topping for pizza.

1. Preheat the oven to 375°F.

2. In a large bowl, whisk together 3 tablespoons of olive oil, the vinegar, the mustard, and ½ teaspoon of salt.

3. Gently toss the broccoli and bell pepper slices in the bowl with the olive oil mixture until they are well coated.

4. Spread the vegetables on a rimmed baking sheet.

5. Add the chicken, the remaining 1 tablespoon of olive oil, and ½ teaspoon of salt to the bowl. Mix until the chicken is well coated and then transfer the chicken to the baking sheet with the broccoli and bell peppers.

6. Bake in the oven for about 20 minutes, or until the chicken is fully cooked and the vegetables are tender.

PREP TIP: Buying broccoli that's already been chopped can save prep and cleanup time.

PER SERVING: Calories: 350; Total fat: 18g; Saturated fat: 3g; Sodium: 760mg; Carbohydrates: 19g; Fiber: 7g; Sugar: 8g; Protein: 31g

CHICKEN SOUVLAKI

GLUTEN-FREE

SERVES 4
PREP TIME: 10 minutes plus 30 minutes to marinate
COOK TIME: 10 minutes

4 boneless, skinless chicken breasts
2 tablespoons extra-virgin olive oil
4 garlic cloves, minced
1 tablespoon dried oregano
1 teaspoon sea salt
½ teaspoon freshly ground black pepper
Juice of 1 large lemon

PER SERVING: Calories: 202; Total fat: 10g; Saturated fat: 2g; Sodium: 636mg; Carbohydrates: 4g; Fiber: 1g; Sugar: 1g; Protein: 26g

Souvlaki is a Greek dish of marinated, skewered, and grilled meat, sometimes accompanied by large chunks of vegetables. This dish has all the flavors of the Mediterranean, which develop and deepen the longer you let it marinate. Ideally, you'd like to marinate the chicken for 8 hours, but even 30 minutes in the refrigerator will produce some amazing flavor and results.

1. Cut the chicken breasts into approximately 1-cubic-inch bite-size pieces.

2. In a large zip-top bag or lidded container, combine the chicken, olive oil, garlic, oregano, salt, pepper, and lemon juice. Toss until the chicken is evenly coated.

3. Close the bag or container and refrigerate for 30 minutes to 8 hours to marinate.

4. Preheat your oven's broiler and place the rack about 5 inches away from the top of the oven. Line a rimmed baking sheet with parchment paper.

5. Place the marinated chicken onto the tray and broil for 6 to 8 minutes, flipping the chicken once while cooking. Remove the chicken when it's no longer pink inside.

PREP TIP: You can also grill the chicken for this recipe. Soak wooden skewers in water for 30 minutes, then thread the chicken breast onto the skewers. Place the skewered chicken onto a preheated, medium-high heat grill for 6 to 8 minutes. Turn the skewers once and cook until the chicken is no longer pink inside.

SPAGHETTI WITH CHICKEN AND CAULIFLOWER

SERVES 4
PREP TIME: 10 minutes
COOK TIME: 20 minutes

4 boneless, skinless
   chicken breasts
1 teaspoon sea
   salt, divided
1 teaspoon freshly ground
   black pepper, divided
4 cups frozen
   cauliflower florets
8 ounces dried
   whole-grain spaghetti
2 teaspoons extra-virgin
   olive oil
1 white onion, diced
3 garlic cloves, minced
Juice of 1 lemon
¾ cup unsweetened
   nondairy milk, divided
⅓ cup Parmesan
   "Cheese" (page 126)

Cooked cauliflower serves as the base for this pasta dish's creamy, dairy-free sauce. To add color, sprinkle the dish with red chili flakes or fresh basil, or stir in some spiralized carrots and cucumber, plus sun-dried tomatoes.

1. Preheat the oven to 375°F.

2. Cut the chicken breasts into 1-inch strips or cubes and season with ½ teaspoon of salt and ½ teaspoon of pepper. Place the chicken on a rimmed baking sheet and cook in the oven for 20 minutes, turning once, while you prepare the rest of the meal.

3. Bring a large pot of water to a boil over high heat and add the frozen cauliflower florets.

4. Boil the cauliflower for 6 to 7 minutes, or until fork-tender. Remove from the heat, drain, and place the cauliflower into a food processor, or blender.

5. Cook the spaghetti according to the package directions.

6. While the pasta is cooking, heat the olive oil in a medium skillet over medium heat and sauté the onion and garlic for about 5 minutes, or until the onion is translucent and fragrant. Add the onion and garlic to the food processor with the cauliflower.

7. Add the lemon juice, ¼ cup of milk, and the remaining ½ teaspoon of salt and ½ teaspoon of pepper to the food processor and blend until smooth, adding more of the milk if the mixture is too thick.

8. Continue to blend until the sauce is creamy.

9. After the spaghetti is cooked and drained, put it back into the pot, add the chicken, and pour in the cauliflower sauce. Mix well.

10. Plate and top with the Parmesan "Cheese."

VARIATION TIP: You can swap out the chicken for baked tofu (see page 72) or tempeh. You can also use gluten-free noodles or other pasta varieties for a different noodle shape.

PER SERVING: Calories: 471; Total fat: 12g; Saturated fat: 2g; Sodium: 706mg; Carbohydrates: 56g; Fiber: 10g; Sugar: 7g; Protein: 41g

Roasted Grape,
Olive, and Tahini Plate,
page **113**

CHAPTER 8

SNACKS, MEZZE, AND SWEETS

GARLIC AND WHITE BEAN DIP

MAKES 2 CUPS
PREP TIME: 10 minutes

1 (16-ounce) can white
   cannellini beans,
   drained and rinsed
Juice of 1 lemon
2 garlic cloves
1 teaspoon dried thyme
¼ cup extra-virgin
   olive oil

I personally love making two to three dips every week when I do my meal preparation, and this recipe is a hit in my house. White bean dip makes a top-notch snack or appetizer and is a great way to sneak in some extra protein during the day. Serve it with cucumber slices, vegetable sticks, and pita, or spread it on tortilla wraps or toast.

1. In a food processor, combine the beans, lemon juice, garlic, thyme, and olive oil and blend.

2. Stop and scrape down the sides of the food processor a few times, then continue blending until smooth. Refrigerate for up to 5 days in an airtight container.

VARIATION TIP: Roast a bulb of garlic by peeling the loose paper skin off, cutting off the top ¼ inch of the garlic bulb, drizzling 1 teaspoon olive oil over it, and roasting it in the oven at 400°F for 45 minutes. Then blend 3 or 4 cloves into the sauce instead of the raw garlic for a richer, mellower flavor, and save the rest of the roasted garlic for other recipes.

PER SERVING (⅓ CUP): Calories: 142; Total fat: 10g; Saturated fat: 1g; Sodium: 24mg; Carbohydrates: 11g; Fiber: 3g; Sugar: 1g; Protein: 4g

OLIVE TAPENADE

GLUTEN-FREE, QUICK

MAKES ½ CUP
PREP TIME: 10 minutes

½ cup kalamata olives
1 tablespoon capers
2 tablespoons coarsely
   chopped fresh parsley
1 tablespoon extra-virgin
   olive oil
1 tablespoon freshly
   squeezed lemon juice
Sea salt

This iconic Mediterranean spread is often found as part of a mezze plate, a selection of small appetizers that's commonly served in Greece and North Africa. It's a simple, tangy dip to go with whole-grain crackers and pita strips.

1. In a food processor, combine the olives, capers, parsley, olive oil, and lemon juice and pulse until the mixture is thick and chunky.

2. Season with salt to taste. Adjust the flavor using more salt and lemon juiceto taste. Leftovers can be kept in the refrigerator for up to 5 days.

PER SERVING (2 TABLESPOONS): Calories: 55; Total fat: 6g; Saturated fat: 1g; Sodium: 199mg; Carbohydrates: 2g; Fiber: 1g; Sugar: <1g; Protein: <1g

SAUERKRAUT AVOCADO MASH

MAKES ⅔ CUP
PREP TIME: 5 minutes

¼ cup sauerkraut,
　chopped
1 medium avocado
Sea salt
Freshly ground
　black pepper

A healthy gut is crucial to feeling your best every day, and this zingy mash makes it easy to eat gut-healing probiotics. Buy your sauerkraut from the refrigerated section of the grocery store to obtain the highest level of probiotics. The avocado helps to tone down the sharpness, while creating a pleasing, smooth texture. Use this mash as a topping for whole-grain toast or salads, in a wrap, or as a dip.

1. In a small bowl, mash together the sauerkraut and avocado.

2. Season with salt and pepper to taste, and enjoy.

VARIATION TIP: Add a powerful nutritional boost, and some extra crunch, by sprinkling ½ tablespoon each of ground flaxseed, chia seeds, hemp hearts, and sesame seeds on top.

PER SERVING (⅓ CUP): Calories: 119; Total fat: 11g; Saturated fat: 2g; Sodium: 200mg; Carbohydrates: 7g; Fiber: 6g; Sugar: 1g; Protein: 2g

ROASTED RED PEPPER AND LENTIL DIP

MAKES 2 CUPS
PREP TIME: 10 minutes

1 (16-ounce) can red
  lentils, drained
  and rinsed
4 ounces roasted red
  peppers, from a jar
Juice of 1 lemon
2 tablespoons extra-virgin
  olive oil
1 tablespoon tahini
1 garlic clove
Sea salt

Keeping a range of healthy snacks in the refrigerator means you're more likely to make smart choices when you get peckish, and this versatile, delicious dip—low in calories but high in protein and iron—is great to have on hand. Serve it with vegetable slices, pita, or tortillas, or use it as an extra protein boost in your sandwiches, wraps, and salads.

1. In a food processor, blend the lentils, roasted red peppers, lemon juice, olive oil, tahini, and garlic until smooth, stopping to scrape down the sides of the bowl as necessary. Season with salt to taste.

2. Refrigerate for up to 5 days in an airtight container.

VARIATION TIP: To make your own roasted red peppers, take 3 red peppers and remove the stems and seeds, cut them in half, and drizzle 1 teaspoon olive oil over each pepper. Roast them in the oven at 450°F for 20 minutes. If you prefer, you can also simmer dried red lentils to go into this dip.

PER SERVING (⅓ CUP): Calories: 129; Total fat: 6g; Saturated fat: 1g; Sodium: 86mg; Carbohydrates: 14g; Fiber: 4g; Sugar: 1g; Protein: 6g

EGYPTIAN-SPICED PITA

QUICK

SERVES 4
PREP TIME: 10 minutes
COOK TIME: 5 minutes

½ cup almonds, dried and unsalted
1 tablespoon sesame seeds
1 tablespoon dried thyme
½ teaspoon fennel seeds
½ teaspoon cumin
½ teaspoon cayenne pepper (optional)
2 whole-grain pitas, cut into triangles
Extra-virgin olive oil

This recipe was inspired by Egyptian dukkah, a crunchy, aromatic mixture of nuts, seeds, and spices that is typically part of a mezze plate. The pita is first dunked in olive oil and then in the mixture, which can also be sprinkled on grilled meats, hummus, egg dishes, avocado, or even radish slices.

1. In a dry, medium skillet over medium-high heat, toast the almonds and sesame seeds for about 4 minutes, or until they begin to brown. Be careful not to burn them.

2. Add the thyme, fennel seeds, cumin, and cayenne pepper (if using) and toast for 1 minute more.

3. Transfer the mixture to a food processor and pulse until a grainy texture forms. Don't over-blend it, or it will begin to become a paste.

4. Serve in a bowl with the divided pitas and a small dish of olive oil for dipping.

5. Store any leftover almond mixture in the refrigerator in an airtight container for up to 2 weeks.

VARIATION TIP: Make this recipe nut-free by swapping out the almonds for sunflower seeds.

PER SERVING: Calories: 297; Total fat: 22g; Saturated fat: 3g; Sodium: 122mg; Carbohydrates: 21g; Fiber: 7g; Sugar: 1g; Protein: 6g

ROASTED GRAPE, OLIVE, AND TAHINI PLATE

GLUTEN-FREE

SERVES 4
PREP TIME: 15 minutes
COOK TIME: 25 minutes

2½ cups seedless
   red grapes
1 tablespoon extra-virgin
   olive oil
2 tablespoons dried
   rosemary
½ cup tahini
½ cup water
1 teaspoon sea salt
1 cup cherry tomatoes
1 cucumber, cut into
   ½-inch-thick slices
1 cup black olives, pitted

Grapes aren't only a sweet snack—they can nicely complement a savory dish. Here, roasted with rosemary, they round out a plate of tahini, olives, and refreshing tomato and cucumber. It's a delightful, surprising combination of flavors and textures.

1. Preheat the oven to 425°F.

2. Toss the grapes in the olive oil and rosemary.

3. On a small rimmed baking sheet, in a single layer, roast the grapes for 25 minutes, stirring halfway through cooking.

4. In a small bowl, whisk together the tahini, water, and salt while the grapes are roasting.

5. Serve the roasted grapes, tomatoes, cucumber slices, and olives with the tahini dip.

VARIATION TIP: Try adding paprika, fresh chives, or diced red onion as a topping on the tahini dip.

PER SERVING: Calories: 341; Total fat: 24g; Saturated fat: 4g; Sodium: 920mg; Carbohydrates: 30g; Fiber: 6g; Sugar: 17g; Protein: 7g

AVOCADO PUDDING

GLUTEN-FREE, QUICK

SERVES 4
PREP TIME: 10 minutes

1 ripe banana

2 avocados

2 tablespoons pure
maple syrup

½ cup unsweetened
nondairy milk

⅓ cup unsweetened
cocoa powder

One of my all-time favorite recipes, this pudding makes a winning snack, but also can be enjoyed for breakfast or dessert. It takes only a few minutes to make, so you can have it ready quickly when those sweet cravings kick in. Healthy fats help balance your blood sugar levels, while the complex carbohydrates provide lasting energy. Feel free to get creative with toppings like unsweetened shredded coconut, chopped nuts, seeds, and fresh fruit.

1. In a food processor, combine the banana, avocados, maple syrup, and milk and blend until smooth, scraping down the sides when necessary.

2. Slowly add the cocoa powder and blend until fully combined.

3. Eat it right after blending, or serve it chilled.

VARIATION TIP: To lower the glycemic index of this recipe, making it an even healthier option for people managing diabetes, use ½ cup pitted Medjool dates that have been soaked and drained in place of the banana.

PER SERVING: Calories: 186; Total fat: 12g; Saturated fat: 2g; Sodium: 30mg; Carbohydrates: 24g; Fiber: 8g; Sugar: 10g; Protein: 3g

APPLE CRISP YOGURT BOWLS

GLUTEN-FREE, QUICK

SERVES 4
PREP TIME: 5 minutes
COOK TIME: 5 to
10 minutes

2 apples, cored and diced
2 cups rolled or quick
   gluten-free oats
¼ cup maple syrup
2 teaspoons cinnamon
1 batch tofu yogurt (see
   page 39)

Yogurt has always been a go-to snack, but adding some fruit and granola can take it to the next level. In this recipe, a simple apple crisp made on the stove top in just a few minutes turns tofu yogurt into dessert (or a treat for breakfast).

1. In a medium saucepan over medium heat, cook the apples, oats, maple syrup, and cinnamon for 6 to 8 minutes, until the apples are golden brown. Stir often so it doesn't burn.

2. Pour the yogurt into bowls and top with the apple crisp.

VARIATION TIP: Use a plant-based, unsweetened yogurt in place of the tofu yogurt and use any variation of your favorite fruits with, or in place of, the apples. One of my favorite alternatives is strawberries with a dash of vanilla extract.

PER SERVING: Calories: 380; Total fat: 6g; Saturated fat: 1g; Sodium: 37mg; Carbohydrates: 77g; Fiber: 8g; Sugar: 38g; Protein: 11g

TAHINI BANANA BOAT

GLUTEN-FREE, QUICK

SERVES 2
PREP TIME: 5 minutes

1 banana
2 tablespoons tahini
1 teaspoon hemp hearts
1 teaspoon ground
   flaxseed
1 teaspoon chia seeds

Balancing the sweetness of the banana with subtly bitter tahini and a crunchy layer of seeds, this combination checks all of the boxes for a healthy snack: simple, satisfying, keeps you full, and reduces cravings. Enjoy it as is or serve with a dish of tofu yogurt (see page 39).

1. Peel the banana and slice in half lengthwise.

2. Drizzle the tahini all over the banana halves and sprinkle the hemp hearts, flaxseed, and chia seeds on top.

VARIATION TIP: To change up the flavors, use 3 teaspoons of any chopped nuts or seeds (such as sunflower seeds, pumpkin seeds, and walnuts) in place of the hemp hearts, flaxseed, and chia seeds.

PER SERVING: Calories: 174; Total fat: 11g; Saturated fat: 1g; Sodium: 18mg; Carbohydrates: 18g; Fiber: 4g; Sugar: 8g; Protein: 5g

STRAWBERRIES WITH MACADAMIA DIP

SERVES 2

PREP TIME: 10 minutes, plus 30 minutes for soaking

½ cup raw
  macadamia nuts
2 teaspoons coconut oil
½ teaspoon cinnamon
1 cup strawberries, hulled

Macadamia nuts are rich in thiamine, which helps the body metabolize glucose and use carbohydrates for energy. These two actions play a key role in blood sugar control, weight management, and heart health, so adding an ounce of macadamia nuts to your diet on a regular basis can have some long-term benefits.

1. Place the macadamia nuts in a bowl and fill it with water. Soak the nuts for 30 minutes to allow them to soften for easier blending. Then drain and rinse the nuts well.

2. In a food processor, blend the nuts and coconut oil until smooth, adding a bit of water as needed to emulsify.

3. Divide the dip between 2 bowls and sprinkle each with ¼ teaspoon cinnamon.

4. Dip the strawberries into the macadamia dip.

PREP TIP: If you don't have 30 minutes to soak the macadamia nuts, cover them in boiling water for 10 minutes, then drain and rinse them well before blending.

PER SERVING: Calories: 307; Total fat: 30g; Saturated fat: 8g; Sodium: 3mg; Carbohydrates: 11g; Fiber: 5g; Sugar: 5g; Protein: 3g

DRIED FIGS AND CASHEW CREAM

GLUTEN-FREE, QUICK

SERVES 2
PREP TIME: 10 minutes

1 cup raw cashews
½ cup water
½ teaspoon
  vanilla extract
1 tablespoon maple syrup
Juice of ¼ lemon
4 dried figs

Cashews have to be one of the most versatile nuts in a plant-based diet. They make a creamy base when blended, so they can be used to make everything from savory soups and tangy "cheese" to this sweet cream that makes a perfect snack or breakfast topping.

1. In a food processor, combine the cashews, water, vanilla, and maple syrup. Blend until the mixture is extremely smooth.

2. Divide the cashew cream between 2 small dessert bowls, add the lemon juice to each dish, and dip the dried figs in the cream.

VARIATION TIP: Buy roasted cashews to add another layer of flavor. You can also use fresh figs instead of dried, and top the cashew cream with any mixture of unsweetened shredded coconut, granola, fruit, seeds, and nuts.

PER SERVING: Calories: 430; Total fat: 29g; Saturated fat: 5g; Sodium: 11mg; Carbohydrates: 38g; Fiber: 4g; Sugar: 18g; Protein: 13g

STAPLES, SAUCES, AND DRESSINGS

HUMMUS

GLUTEN-FREE, QUICK

MAKES 2 CUPS
PREP TIME: 10 minutes

1 (16-ounce) can
   chickpeas, drained
   and rinsed
1 garlic clove
Juice of 1 lemon
1 teaspoon sea salt
⅓ cup tahini
¼ cup extra-virgin olive
   oil, divided

A staple of the Mediterranean diet that's gone global, hummus is made from blended chickpeas, garlic, lemon juice, tahini, and olive oil. Rich in protein, iron, and flavor, it's not only for snacking with pita and vegetables, but for layering onto sandwiches, wraps, and salads, and topping salmon or cooked chicken.

1. In a food processor, combine the chickpeas, garlic, lemon juice, salt, and tahini and blend until smooth. You may have to stop and scrape down the sides of the bowl a few times.

2. Drizzle 3 tablespoons of olive oil into the food processor as it blends to create a light, airy hummus.

3. Remove the hummus from the food processor and transfer to an airtight container. Pour the remaining 1 tablespoon of olive oil over the top to keep it fresh. Refrigerate for up to 5 days.

VARIATION TIP: You can omit the garlic and lemon juice and swap out the olive oil for ¼ cup of unsweetened nondairy milk plus ¼ cup of unsweetened cocoa powder for a chocolate dessert hummus. Pair it with your favorite fruits.

PER SERVING (⅓ CUP): Calories: 222; Total fat: 17g; Saturated fat: 2g; Sodium: 499mg; Carbohydrates: 14g; Fiber: 4g; Sugar: 2g; Protein: 5g

VEGETABLE BROTH

GLUTEN-FREE

MAKES 6 CUPS
PREP TIME: 15 minutes
COOK TIME: 40 minutes

2 celery stalks
2 large carrots
1 large onion
1 tablespoon extra-virgin
  olive oil
8 garlic cloves, minced
2 tablespoons
  dried parsley
2 tablespoons
  dried thyme
2 bay leaves
8 cups water

Since store-bought vegetable broth tends to be high in sodium and preservatives, it's best to make your own—which is not only easy but offers a catch-all way to repurpose veggie scraps before throwing them away. I use my vegetable stocks to sauté vegetables when I want to reduce my use of oils, make soups, and cook quinoa and other grains.

1. Under cool running water, scrub the celery and carrots clean with a brush. You do not need to peel the carrots.

2. Remove the skin from the onion and then coarsely chop the celery, carrots, and onion into 1-inch chunks.

3. In a large stockpot over high heat, heat the olive oil. Add the chopped vegetables, the garlic, parsley, thyme, and bay leaves. Cook for about 5 minutes, or until the garlic is fragrant.

4. Add the water, stir well, and bring to a boil. Once the pot is boiling, turn the heat to low and simmer, uncovered, for 30 minutes.

Continued >

5. Strain the liquid and discard the solids.

6. Allow the vegetable stock to cool before transferring to jars for the refrigerator or zip-top bags for the freezer.

INGREDIENT TIP: The broth can be stored in the refrigerator for up to 5 days or in the freezer for several months. If you're storing it in the freezer, use zip-top bags on a baking tray, as they can lie flat while the broth freezes. After the broth has frozen solid, you can store it either flat or standing upright.

PREP TIP: Keep a bag of vegetable scraps in your freezer, then use 2 cups of vegetable scraps to make your broth, instead of using fresh, whole vegetables. This helps repurpose the scraps and saves you money. Mushroom stems, broccoli stems, wilted spinach, kale, Swiss chard leaves, eggplant ends, and bell pepper ends can all go in the pot.

PER SERVING (½ CUP): Calories: 21; Total fat: 1g; Saturated fat: <1g; Sodium: 9mg; Carbohydrates: 3g; Fiber: 1g; Sugar: 1g; Protein: <1g

SLOW BATCH-COOKED BEANS

GLUTEN-FREE

MAKES 10 CUPS
PREP TIME: 5 minutes, plus 12 hours for soaking
COOK TIME: 3 to 6 hours

4 cups dried beans, single variety
4 quarts water, divided
2 teaspoons salt
¼ cup apple cider vinegar (optional)

PER SERVING (½ CUP): Calories: 128; Total fat: 2g; Saturated fat: 0g; Sodium: 244mg; Carbohydrates: 22g; Fiber: 6g; Sugar: 4g; Protein: 7g

Buying canned beans is great for convenience, but you can save a lot of money by buying dried beans in bulk and cooking them yourself. Dry beans can take a long time to rehydrate and cook, so the trick is to make them in large batches. Use this recipe for any kind of bean—including kidney beans, white cannellini beans, black turtle beans, and romano beans.

1. Pick through your beans for any small rocks and dried plant debris, then in a large soup pot, soak the beans overnight, for 8 to 12 hours, in 2 quarts of water. They will have doubled in size after this time. Drain and rinse them well.

2. Add the beans to the slow cooker with the remaining 2 quarts of water and the salt.

3. Cook on high for 3 to 4 hours, or on low for 5 to 6 hours.

4. Check after 3 (or 5) hours for doneness. If the beans are firm or crunchy, cook for another hour. The beans are done when they're soft, but not mushy.

5. Add the vinegar (if using) and stir well.

6. Allow the beans to cool, and then store in an airtight container in the refrigerator for up to 5 days, or in zip-top bags in the freezer for several months.

INGREDIENT TIP: The apple cider vinegar helps to disable and deactivate the digestive sugars in beans that can cause gas and bloating for some people. Use it if beans tend to give you some digestive discomfort.

VARIATION TIP: You can follow this same cooking method with whole grains, such as wild rice, farro, spelt, buckwheat, or barley, but skip the soaking, as it's not necessary.

PARMESAN "CHEESE"

GLUTEN-FREE, QUICK

MAKES ⅔ CUP
PREP TIME: 5 minutes

¼ cup hemp hearts
¼ cup raw cashews
¼ cup nutritional yeast
1 teaspoon garlic powder

This dairy-free take on Parmesan cheese makes a fantastic, subtly-flavored topping for pasta dishes, salads, and casseroles. It also adds a huge nutritional boost to your meals without compromising on flavor or texture.

1. In a small blender or food processor, combine the hemp hearts, cashews, nutritional yeast, and garlic powder and blitz quickly until the mixture resembles grated Parmesan. Careful not to blend too long, or the cashews will become cashew butter.

2. Store in an airtight container and keep refrigerated for up to 2 weeks.

INGREDIENT TIP: Consider buying nutritional yeast that has been fortified with vitamin B12 to help ensure you're getting your daily dose requirements typically obtained from meat and eggs.

VARIATION TIP: Make this recipe nut-free by replacing the cashews with shelled, raw sunflower seeds. The result will be a drier, flakier version of the cheese, but you can add a teaspoon of extra-virgin olive oil to the blender to soften the texture.

PER SERVING (2 TABLESPOONS): Calories: 98; Total fat: 6g; Saturated fat: 1g; Sodium: 3mg; Carbohydrates: 5g; Fiber: 2g; Sugar: <1g; Protein: 7g

SOFT "CHEESE" SPREAD

GLUTEN-FREE, QUICK

MAKES 1 CUP
PREP TIME: 10 minutes
COOK TIME: 10 minutes

1 cup raw cashews
2 cups water, divided
1 garlic clove, minced
¼ cup nutritional yeast
2 tablespoons apple
   cider vinegar

PER SERVING (¼ CUP):
Calories: 212; Total fat: 15g;
Saturated fat: 3g; Sodium:
7mg; Carbohydrates:
13g; Fiber: 3g; Sugar: 2g;
Protein: 10g

When I first made the switch to plant-based eating, I had a really difficult time giving up cheese. It was definitely my comfort food when I had cravings, felt too lazy to make a real meal, or needed something quick on the go. Cream cheese fell into this category for me and was something that I missed terribly when I finally made the full transition. This dairy-free spread offers me huge comfort on a regular basis.

1. In a small pot over high heat, boil the cashews in 1 cup of water for about 10 minutes, or until the cashews are soft.

2. Drain and rinse the cashews really well before adding them to a food processor with the garlic, nutritional yeast, and vinegar.

3. Blend the ingredients until smooth, scraping the sides of the bowl as needed and adding small amounts of water, 1 tablespoon at a time, if necessary.

4. Transfer to an airtight container and let it sit in the refrigerator for 1 hour to deepen the flavors, or serve it as is.

INGREDIENT TIP: If you'd like a stronger cheese flavor, feel free to blend in 2 teaspoons of white miso paste.

VARIATION TIP: I love making an herb and garlic cream cheese by adding ½ teaspoon oregano, ½ teaspoon basil, ½ teaspoon parsley, and ¼ teaspoon dried dill. You can also make this into a cheese ball by adding 2 tablespoons refined coconut oil to the food processor and then storing the cheese wrapped in plastic wrap for 1 hour in the refrigerator to firm up.

PERFECT PESTO

GLUTEN-FREE, QUICK

MAKES 1 CUP
PREP TIME: 10 minutes

1 cup fresh basil leaves
¼ cup sunflower
   seeds, shelled
1 garlic clove
¼ cup extra-virgin
   olive oil
1 tablespoon freshly
   squeezed lemon juice
¼ cup Parmesan
   "Cheese" (page 126)

Traditionally, pesto is made with pine nuts and Parmesan cheese. We're going to make this dairy-free recipe with a few basic pantry staples, including sunflower seeds in place of the pine nuts so that you have some alternative ways to use what you have in stock.

In a food processor, combine the basil, sunflower seeds, garlic, olive oil, and Parmesan "Cheese" and blend until smooth. Refrigerate in an airtight container for up to 3 days.

VARIATION TIP: If you cannot find fresh basil, use spinach and about 2 tablespoons dried basil. As a substitute for the Parmesan "Cheese," use 2 tablespoons nutritional yeast for a similar flavor.

PER SERVING (¼ CUP): Calories: 224; Total fat: 21g; Saturated fat: 3g; Sodium: 3mg; Carbohydrates: 5g; Fiber: 2g; Sugar: 1g; Protein: 6g

STRAWBERRY-CHIA JAM

MAKES 1 CUP
PREP TIME: 15 minutes

2 cups strawberries
2 tablespoons chia seeds
1 tablespoon freshly
    squeezed lemon juice
1 tablespoon maple syrup
    (optional)

Supermarket jams can be loaded with unnecessary amounts of refined sugars, and the fruits have often been so heavily processed and boiled that they lose their nutrients. While keeping in line with a healthy diet, this bright, simple jam recipe comes together quickly and still packs a lot of nutrition. I like to have one or two flavors on hand at all times, and keep costs low by using frozen berries when they're not in season.

1. Hull the strawberries and add the fruit to a blender.

2. Pulse the strawberries a few times to break them up, then add the chia seeds, lemon juice, and maple syrup, if using.

3. Pulse a few more times, until the mixture is well combined and mostly smooth. A few remaining chunks of fruit are okay.

4. Pour the jam into an airtight container and allow it to set for 10 minutes in the refrigerator. Use within 7 days.

INGREDIENT TIP: You can skip the lemon juice if you're using a very tart fruit, such as raspberries or pineapple, and you may have to adjust the maple syrup, as well. Try not to add more than 2 tablespoons of maple syrup to this recipe to keep the added sugars to a minimum.

VARIATION TIP: You can use any juicy fruit in this recipe to make the jam. Some of my favorites are blueberries, raspberries, kiwi, pineapples, cherries, peaches, plums, and apricots.

PER SERVING (2 TABLESPOONS): Calories: 28; Total fat: 1g; Saturated fat: 0g; Sodium: <1mg; Carbohydrates: 4g; Fiber: 2g; Sugar: 2g; Protein: 1g

TZATZIKI

GLUTEN-FREE, QUICK

**MAKES APPROXIMATELY
2 CUPS**

PREP TIME: 15 minutes

½ cucumber

2 garlic cloves

14 ounces medium-firm
  tofu, drained

2 tablespoons extra-virgin
  olive oil

Juice of ½ lemon

1 teaspoon apple
  cider vinegar

1 teaspoon dried dill

Sea salt

Freshly ground
  black pepper

Tzatziki is traditionally made from Greek yogurt, cucumbers, and fresh herbs. This dairy-free version is close to the original in its flavor and texture, gaining its creaminess from tofu. Serve it in sandwiches and wraps, on salads and grilled meats, or as a dip for pita and vegetables.

1. Slice the cucumber lengthwise. Scoop out the seeds and discard them. Shred the cucumber using a box shredder, then squeeze out any excess liquid and set the shredded cucumber aside.

2. In a food processor, pulse the garlic a few times to mince the cloves.

3. Add the tofu, olive oil, lemon juice, vinegar, dill, and salt and pepper to taste to the food processor. Blend until smooth.

4. Add the shredded cucumber to the food processor and blitz a few times to incorporate. Refrigerate in an airtight container for up to 4 days.

VARIATION TIP: Use ⅔ cup cashews plus ½ cup water instead of the tofu to make a soy-free version.

PER SERVING (⅓ CUP): Calories: 108; Total fat: 8g; Saturated fat: 1g; Sodium: 5mg; Carbohydrates: 3g; Fiber: 1g; Sugar: 1g; Protein: 7g

TAHINI DRESSING

GLUTEN-FREE, QUICK

MAKES 1 CUP
PREP TIME: 10 minutes

¼ cup extra-virgin
    olive oil
¼ cup freshly squeezed
    lemon juice
¼ cup tahini
1 cup fresh cilantro,
    coarsely chopped
Sea salt

Store-bought salad dressings are sometimes loaded with unhealthy ingredients, and the calories can add up very quickly. But you can make your own dressings at home with the ingredients that you have on hand in the pantry. Toss this dressing with a salad, such as the Charred Kale Salad (page 53), pour over falafel, or add to sandwiches and wraps.

1. In a food processor or blender, combine the olive oil, lemon juice, tahini, and cilantro, and blend until the dressing is smooth and takes on a gentle green color.

2. Season with salt to taste.

VARIATION TIP: Use lime juice or apple cider vinegar if you don't have any lemons or lemon juice on hand. Also, not everyone is a fan of fresh cilantro; you can swap it out for equal amounts of fresh parsley.

PER SERVING (¼ CUP): Calories: 213; Total fat: 22g; Saturated fat: 3g; Sodium: 20mg; Carbohydrates: 4g; Fiber: 2g; Sugar: 1g; Protein: 3g

SUMAC DRESSING

GLUTEN-FREE, QUICK

MAKES ½ CUP
PREP TIME: 5 minutes

¼ cup extra-virgin
  olive oil
¼ cup maple syrup
1 tablespoon freshly
  squeezed lemon juice
1 teaspoon sea salt
2 tablespoons
  ground sumac

Sumac is a common spice in the Middle East, used on grilled meats, rice, and vegetables. It adds a wonderful, aromatic depth to this simple dressing. I usually make it in a small mason jar when I'm preparing for the week, as it motivates me to eat more vegetables and salads. You can make this in a repurposed sauce jar, or even just a small bowl with a lid.

1. In a small mason jar, combine the olive oil, maple syrup, lemon juice, salt, and sumac and put the lid on.

2. Shake until well-combined. Refrigerate for up to 1 week in an airtight container.

VARIATION TIP: Use apple cider vinegar or red wine vinegar in place of the lemon juice.

PER SERVING (1 TABLESPOON): Calories: 93; Total fat: 7g; Saturated fat: 1g; Sodium: 322mg; Carbohydrates: 8g; Fiber: 1g; Sugar: 6g; Protein: <1g

MEASUREMENT CONVERSIONS

VOLUME EQUIVALENTS	U.S. STANDARD	U.S. STANDARD (OUNCES)	METRIC (APPROXIMATE)
LIQUID	2 tablespoons	1 fl. oz.	30 mL
	¼ cup	2 fl. oz.	60 mL
	½ cup	4 fl. oz.	120 mL
	1 cup	8 fl. oz.	240 mL
	1½ cups	12 fl. oz.	355 mL
	2 cups or 1 pint	16 fl. oz.	475 mL
	4 cups or 1 quart	32 fl. oz.	1 L
	1 gallon	128 fl. oz.	4 L
DRY	⅛ teaspoon	—	0.5 mL
	¼ teaspoon	—	1 mL
	½ teaspoon	—	2 mL
	¾ teaspoon	—	4 mL
	1 teaspoon	—	5 mL
	1 tablespoon	—	15 mL
	¼ cup	—	59 mL
	⅓ cup	—	79 mL
	½ cup	—	118 mL
	⅔ cup	—	156 mL
	¾ cup	—	177 mL
	1 cup	—	235 mL
	2 cups or 1 pint	—	475 mL
	3 cups	—	700 mL
	4 cups or 1 quart	—	1 L
	½ gallon	—	2 L
	1 gallon	—	4 L

OVEN TEMPERATURES

FAHRENHEIT	CELSIUS (APPROXIMATE)
250°F	120°C
300°F	150°C
325°F	165°C
350°F	180°C
375°F	190°C
400°F	200°C
425°F	220°C
450°F	230°C

WEIGHT EQUIVALENTS

U.S. STANDARD	METRIC (APPROXIMATE)
½ ounce	15 g
1 ounce	30 g
2 ounces	60 g
4 ounces	115 g
8 ounces	225 g
12 ounces	340 g
16 ounces or 1 pound	455 g

RESOURCES

If you're looking for more information, resources, and recipes for plant-based eating, I strongly recommend having a look at the websites of numerous leading physicians who advocate the safe and enjoyable adoption of the plant-based diet.

Trusted sources of science-backed information include:

Dr. Michael Gregor, MD, FACLM, well-known author of *How Not to Die*, maintains a simple-to-use website full of videos, webinars, a podcast, and a blog. You can find his book and information here: NutritionFacts.org.

Dr. Caldwell Esselstyn, Jr., MD, surgeon and author of *Prevent and Reverse Heart Disease*, has been a leader in the science of plant-based eating since 1984. Find more information, FAQs, and videos here: DrEsselstyn.com.

The book and documentary *Forks Over Knives* has made worldwide waves in the study of nutrition and its effects on our long-term health. It features the research of Dr. T. Colin Campbell, author of more than 300 peer-reviewed research papers, who maintains a beautiful website with lots of plant-based resources. Have fun diving into the plethora of tasty recipes here: ForksOverKnives.com/recipes.

The American Heart Association advocates strongly for the Mediterranean diet and offers plenty of tips and infographics so you can adopt it into your lifestyle. Learn more here: Heart.org/en/healthy-living/healthy-eating /eat-smart/nutrition-basics/mediterranean-diet.

Depending on your region, some ingredients for a plant-based diet can be a little bit difficult to come by but can make the difference between a meal that's drab or fab. There's almost nothing that can't be found online these days, so if you can't find the ingredients at your local grocery store, here are some of the brands I use and love:

» Bob's Red Mill Nutritional Yeast Flakes
» Hikari Organic White Miso Paste
» Manitoba Harvest Organic Shelled Hemp Hearts
» Viva Naturals Organic Raw Chia Seeds

REFERENCES

Academy of Nutrition and Dietetics. "Processed Foods: What's Okay and What to Avoid." Eat Right. February 11, 2019. Updated February 2020. EatRight.org/food/nutrition/nutrition-facts-and-food-labels/processed-foods-whats-ok-and-what-to-avoid.

BBC. "What Should I Eat for a Healthy Gut?" Accessed February 5, 2021. BBC.co.uk/food/articles/what_should_you_eat_for_a_healthy_gut.

The Bean Institute. "Bean Nutrition Overview." Accessed February 6, 2020. BeanInstitute.com/bean-nutrition-overview.

Benioff Children's Hospitals. "Why Fiber Is So Good for You." UCSF. Accessed February 3, 2021. UCSFBenioffChildrens.org/education/why_fiber_is_so_good_for_you.

Bradford, Alina. "How Blue LEDs Affect Sleep." Live Science. February 27, 2016. LiveScience.com/53874-blue-light-sleep.html.

Brazier, Yvette. "What Are the Health Benefits of Olive Oil?" Medical News Today. December 18, 2019. MedicalNewsToday.com/articles/266258#what-is-olive-oil.

Cleveland Clinic. "Gut-Brain Connection." December 3, 2020. my.ClevelandClinic.org/health/treatments/16358-gut-brain-connection.

Cleveland Clinic. "The Best (and Worst) Diets If You Have Diabetes." December 22, 2016.health.ClevelandClinic.org/3-best-and-3-worst-diets-to-try-when-you-have-diabetes.

Coughlin, Jovina. "History of Panini." Jovina Cooks. August 3, 2015. JovinaCooksItalian.com/tag/history-of-panini.

David, Elizabeth. *Italian Food*. London: Barrie & Jenkins, 1990.

Environmental Working Group. "Dirty Dozen™." Accessed February 6, 2021. EWG.org/foodnews/dirty-dozen.php.

Forks Over Knives. "How a Plant-Based Diet Can Boost Your Health." January 3, 2017. Updated December 21, 2020. ForksOverKnives.com/how-tos/plant-based-primer-beginners-guide-starting-plant-based-diet/#.

Fox, Maggie. "The Real Brain Food Could Be Fresh Veggies and Olive Oil, Study Finds." Today. January 4, 2017. Today.com/health/mediterranean-diet -could-save-your-brain-study-finds-t106694.

Gunnars, Kris. "Mediterranean Diet 101: A Meal Plan and Beginner's Guide." Healthline. July 24, 2018. Healthline.com/nutrition/mediterranean-diet -meal-plan#the-basics.

Harvard Health Publishing. "Becoming a Vegetarian." Harvard Medical School. April 2010. Updated April 15, 2020. Health.Harvard.edu/staying-healthy /becoming-a-vegetarian.

Harvard Health Publishing. "Quick-Start Guide to Nuts and Seeds." Harvard Medical School. September 2019. Health.Harvard.edu/staying-healthy /quick-start-guide-to-nuts-and-seeds.

Harvard T.H. Chan School of Public Health. "Fiber." Accessed February 3, 2021. HSPH.Harvard.edu/nutritionsource/carbohydrates/fiber.

Harvard T.H. Chan School of Public Health. "Processed Foods and Health." Accessed February 1, 2021. HSPH.Harvard.edu/nutritionsource/processed-foods.

Head to Health. "Purposeful Activities—Hobbies." Australian Government Department of Health. July 11, 2019. HeadToHealth.gov.au/meaningful-life /purposeful-activity/hobbies.

Hirotsu, Camila et al. "Interactions between Sleep, Stress, and Metabolism: From Physiological to Pathological Conditions." *Sleep Science* vol. 8, no. 3 (2015): 143–52. doi:10.1016/j.slsci.2015.09.002 NCBI.NLM.NIH.gov/pmc/articles /PMC4688585.

Holohan, Meghan. "What Is The Best Diet for 2020? Mediterranean, Flexitarian and DASH Top List." Today. January 2, 2020. Today.com/health/what-best -diet-2020-mediterranean-flexitarian-dash-top-list-t170697.

Hunnes, Dana. "The Case for Plant-Based Diet." UCLA Sustainability. Accessed February 1, 2021. Sustain.UCLA.edu/our-initiatives/food-systems/the-case-for -plant-based.

Kubala, Jillian. "9 Impressive Health Benefits of Onions." Healthline. December 18, 2018. Healthline.com/nutrition/onion-benefits.

Long Island Weight Loss Institute. "Surprising Health Benefits of Getting Fresh Air." May 28, 2020. LIWLI.com/surprising-health-benefits-of-fresh-air.

Mayo Clinic. "Vitamin A." November 13, 2020. MayoClinic.org/drugs-supplements -vitamin-a/art-20365945.

Norwegian University of Science and Technology. "Feed Your Genes: How Our Genes Respond to the Foods We Eat." Science Daily. September 20, 2011. ScienceDaily.com/releases/2011/09/110919073845.htm.

Raman, Ryan. "14 Healthy Whole-Grain Foods (Including Gluten-Free Options)." Healthline. July 14, 2018. Healthline.com/nutrition/whole-grain-foods#TOC _TITLE_HDR_3.

Stanford Children's Health. "Why the Family Meal Is Important." Accessed February 7, 2021. StanfordChildrens.org/en/topic/default?id=why-the -family-meal-is-important-1-701.

Thurrot, Stephanie. "The Mediterranean Diet Is Consistently Ranked 1 of the Best. Here's Why." Today. October 15, 2020. Today.com/health/what-mediterranean -diet-diet-meal-plan-explained-t194816.

Tsaban G, Yaskolka Meir A, Rinott E, et al. "The Effect of Green Mediterranean Diet on Cardiometabolic Risk: A Randomised Controlled Trial." (Published online ahead of print, November 23, 2020.) *Heart*. DOI:10.1136/heartjnl-2020 -317802pubmed.ncbi.nlm.nih.gov/33234670.

Ware, Megan. "Why Do We Need Magnesium?" Medical News Today. January 6, 2020. MedicalNewsToday.com/articles/286839.

World Health Organization. "The Top 10 Causes of Death." December 9, 2020. WHO.int/news-room/fact-sheets/detail/the-top-10-causes-of-death.

INDEX

Acknowledgments

I would like to thank the many people in my life who have helped shape me into a leader. My parents, who have always believed in my unlimited potential, and who gifted me with my nutrition programs, making it possible to become a nutritionist. My incredible friends at Team Vision, who have helped me meet challenges and step into a better version of myself. And lastly, my husband and daughter, who remind me every single day that the most important things we can have in life are our freedom, our health, and the love of our family. Without their support, understanding, and unconditional love, this book would not have been possible.

I am forever grateful for the amazing people I have crossed paths with in my journey thus far, and look forward to the many more that I have yet to meet.

About the Author

 **Jenn Jodouin,** born and raised in Northern Ontario, Canada, is an advanced holistic hormone health nutritionist with training in seven different areas of nutrition. "One Bite at a Time" isn't just her coaching motto—it's how she's been able to overcome crippling health and hormone challenges that impacted her quality of life. Navigating the health care system presented obstacles that motivated Jenn to look for answers, solutions, and preventative options to her problems. This led her to discover the world of plant-based diets, the healing powers they offer, and to enjoy a life of good health, energy, and vibrancy! This plant-based mama's mission is to save others from similar frustration and pain by shining a light on the simplicity and healing properties of shifting one's nutrition and lifestyle. In her free time, Jenn enjoys spending time with her family outdoors hiking, canoeing, camping, biking, and gardening.

CPSIA information can be obtained
at www.ICGtesting.com
Printed in the USA
JSHW022112070821
17583JS00002B/4